# A2 MEDIA STUDIES:

## THE ESSENTIAL REVISION GUIDE FOR AQA

*A2 Media Studies: The Essential Revision Guide for AQA* is the must-have, self-help resource for students preparing for AQA A2 Media Studies exams.

Individual sections cover the following key topics:

- **Texts and Contexts in the Media (MED4)**
- The Production and Manufacture of News
- Representations
- Genre
- Media Audiences

- **Comparative Critical Analysis (MED6)**
- Texts
- Making Connections
- Wider Contexts
- Theoretical Perspectives

Written by experienced teachers and examiners, *A2 Media Studies: The Essential Revision Guide for AQA* provides invaluable advice and support and includes:

- Activities
- Exam questions
- Worked examples
- Revision tips

- How does the exam system work?
- Suggested resources

# A2 MEDIA STUDIES:

## THE ESSENTIAL REVISION GUIDE FOR AQA

Jo Barker and Peter Wall

Routledge
Taylor & Francis Group

LONDON AND NEW YORK

First published 2006
by Routledge
2 Park Square, Milton Park, Abingdon, Oxon OX14 4RN

Simultaneously published in the USA and Canada
by Taylor & Francis Inc
270 Madison Ave, New York, NY10016

*Routledge is an imprint of the Taylor & Francis Group*

Typeset in Trade Gothic and Univers by
Keystroke, Jacaranda Lodge, Wolverhampton
Printed and bound in Great Britain by
Bell & Bain Ltd, Glasgow

*British Library Cataloguing in Publication Data*
A catalogue record for this book is available from the British Library

*Library of Congress Cataloging in Publication Data*
A catalog record for this book has been requested

ISBN10: 0–415–36565–1 (hbk)
ISBN10: 0–415–36566–X (pbk)
ISBN10: 0–203–96978–2 (ebk)

ISBN13: 9–78–0–415–36565–9 (hbk)
ISBN13: 9–78–0–415–36566–6 (pbk)
ISBN13: 9–78–0–203–96978–6 (ebk)

302.23052

302.23054

A0046534
£9.99
27/11/06

# CONTENTS

# CONCLUSION 139

# APPENDIX 143

# INTRODUCTION

# THE CHALLENGE OF A2

So you have managed to get this far – well done!! The good news is that you have probably done the hard bit in getting through the AS component of the course. The A2 bit should be comparatively plain sailing.

So what is A2 all about? Well in essence it develops the skills that you learned at AS so that you are able to apply them with a greater degree of sophistication than you were in the first year of your course. Of course, you may well think that you didn't really develop any skills doing AS other than your ability to pass exams. This is a good point, therefore, at which to look back over the work you did for AS and make an audit of the skills that you developed. These can be summarised as follows:

1   A grasp of the key concepts that informed a great deal of your AS work

2   The ability to analyse texts using these key concepts

3   Production skills in creating your media product for MED3

4   Evaluative skills in terms of both your own productions and mass media output

NOTE

With any luck you will have remembered the key concepts. Just in case you have had such a good summer that you have forgotten, here is a brief summary of them.

■ Representations
■ Media language – genre and narrative
■ Values and ideology

■ Institutions
■ Audience

In addition to the Media Studies skills that you developed above, your first year of study should also have taught you a lot of other skills that are going to come in particularly handy for tackling A2. These skills include:

1    Study skills. You will have learned how to study and the particular approaches that are most effective in studying the media. There is a section reminding you of these on page 15.

2    Research skills. These are going to become especially important at A2 level as you develop more and more independence in your learning.

3    Essay writing skills. Remember the skill you developed for MED1 and MED2 about writing essays under exam conditions. You are going to need those again.

4    Your ability to work autonomously. Remember, that means your ability (and willingness) to go off on your own and explore both media texts and the issues that they raise.

This is a good point at which to subject yourself to a 'swot' analysis. SWOT stands for:

- *Strengths*

- *Weaknesses*

- *Opportunities*

- *Threats*

So a SWOT analysis is about standing back for a moment and making an honest assessment of what you have achieved and what you need to do to achieve even more. So using the two lists above, try identifying under these headings just what are the strengths and weaknesses you have exhibited and what opportunities and threats might result from these. Put more simply, identify the things you think you are good at and those that you think you are not so good at.

Of course it is no good just leaving it at that. The things you are good at present opportunities. For example, if you think you are good at research skills, A2 will provide you with lots of opportunities for developing these skills beyond the immediate confines of Media Studies as well as into wider contexts which we look at in a moment. More importantly, you need to confront any perceived weaknesses in your skills base. It is no good being brilliant at research if you can't write essays. The two go hand in hand. If you can't write essays, then seek help from someone who can help you. At the very least take time to read the sections covering exam technique in this book and its companion Bennett, P., Slater, S. and Wall, P., (2005) *A2 Media Studies: The Essential Introduction*, London: Routledge.

## SO HOW IS A2 DIFFERENT FROM AS?

The whole AQA GCE Media Studies qualification relies heavily on ideas centred around the analysis of media texts. The units at A2 are no exception. Textual analysis and the application of the key concepts to this analysis remain absolutely central to your success or failure. You do need, however, to be aware of two new dimensions that have an impact on the way in which A2 units are assessed. These are:

1 wider contexts

2 theoretical perspectives

You will read a good deal more about these as we look closely at the demands of the externally assessed units, MED4 and MED6. It is useful though to take a brief look at them here so you can get thinking about how you are going to deal with them.

## WIDER CONTEXTS

Media texts do not exist in a vacuum, even though exam boards like to encapsulate them into exam papers and make you analyse them. Media texts are both created and consumed as part of a complex social and cultural organisation in which we live. Media texts both reflect and influence the society and culture they exist in. This is one reason that Media Studies is not only interesting but also important. The nature of media texts, the output of media institutions and the consumption of media audiences all provide important barometers of the concerns, values and neuroses of the culture in which we live. Studying the media is, therefore, one way of gaining valuable insight into the very nature of culture and some would argue the state of its health.

So wider contexts as they relate to A2 are the cultural and social conditions that exist at a time a media text is produced and consumed.

> **NOTE**
>
> Why is there so much reality television on our screens? Possible answers:
>
> - That's what people want to watch.
> - Producers find it cheap to make and have the production facilities, such as the Big Brother house, set up ready to use.
> - Society is sick and voyeuristic and enjoys seeing the pain and suffering of others.
> - In the digital age there are just so many hours of air time to fill, so broadcasters like any programme that is cheap and fills up huge amounts of this air time.
> - Bad television is just so ironic.

Notice none of these answers is directly related to reality television texts. Each offers a wider context, either in terms of production, audience consumption or the nature of our culture and society. So when you are asked to explore 'wider contexts' as part of your A2 course, this is the sort of area you need to be looking at: the contexts of production and consumption as well as the broader cultural and social contexts that influence the nature of a media text and in turn are likely to be influenced by it.

Hang on to the stuff about irony – you may want to think about that later.

> **NOTE**
>
> One of the aims of the specification is:
>
> To develop candidates' ability to explore the historical, social, political and economic contexts relevant to the critical reading of media texts and an understanding of media issues.

You may have noticed a problem. In a nutshell – how am I supposed to get at these wider contexts? You may have noticed an even bigger problem. How am I supposed to write about these wider contexts in an exam when it will be the first time I have seen these texts?

Well of course there is no simple answer to either question. The first is probably the easier of the two. You need to do some research. That means you need to do a little bit of digging around to get to the background information that you need about texts and issues you are exploring.

Fortunately there is something built into the specification to help you. It is called MED5, Independent Study. By the time you read this you will probably know a fair bit about it. You will know that you are expected to take a contemporary media issue and produce a 3,000-word study of it. Following the guidance in the specification, you will appreciate that this is a text based study, i.e. it has to be rooted in some element of media text as its starting point. What you are then expected to do is to work outwards from the text in order to access wider contexts of the type we explored above.

With any luck you will be reading this before you embark on your Independent Study. If you have already completed Unit 5, all is not lost, however. Your choice of topic for the Independent Study unit can have key bearing on what you need to do to prepare for your externally assessed units, especially MED4. It can help specifically by enabling you to do some background research into at least one of the topics you are preparing for in MED4. This is where you need to enter into a discussion with the teacher who is supervising your Independent Study and the teacher who is preparing you for the MED4 exam, if these are not the same person.

An obvious example might be focusing on some aspect of news-gathering and presentation of news or your MED5 topic so that you have ready-prepared material for use in the MED4 exam. Similarly most media texts you look at are likely to raise issues of representation and genre, so you should see here a potential overlap with one or both of these MED4 topic areas.

## THEORETICAL PERSPECTIVES

Your study of the media should have made you aware of the vast extent to which it is used socially. Media output is a common talking point whenever people meet and exchange ideas. Just about everyone has something to say about the media, especially contemporary topics such as the latest reality TV show or a controversial new film showing at the cinema. On this basis, the majority of the population could wander into a media studies exam room and have a go at many of the questions on the paper. Some of the better informed might even scrape a pass. The reason that they would probably fail, however, is that their knowledge and understanding of the media would lack the important theoretical framework that is central to an academic study of the media. It is this theoretical base that you need to be able to demonstrate that is an important ingredient of your success at A2.

Of course at this point you are hoping for a list of key theories that you can learn and show off in the exam. You have probably guessed, however, that being Media

Studies it is not quite that simple. There is a list coming up you will be glad to hear but it is not the sort of thing that you can just learn and trot out in the exam. Let's try to explain why.

The history of cultural studies, the larger discipline of which Media Studies is a part, is littered with theories many of which are now quite outmoded not least because of changes in the way technology has influenced the production and consumption of media texts. Roughly we can identify a continuum running from the early propaganda models of the Frankfurt School through to postmodern notions of media and personal identity. Most theories by their nature are designed to explore texts and issues from a specific point of view. Far from being an objective take, they seek to put forward and support a particular perspective from which to consider media output. A good example of this would be feminist theory.

Feminist theory sees the media and its texts from the perspective of women. Clearly this is a complex issue, but at a simple level many media texts can be interpreted through their ideological function of supporting and preserving the patriarchal social order in which power is vested in men. Media texts can be seen as a mechanism for controlling women in order to ensure they remain in a position in society which is subordinate to men. A survey of advertising for example by a feminist would point to the representation of women in advertisements in a comparatively limited number of roles compared to those represented by men. The conclusion might be that the media do this in order to gain our acceptance that this is natural or inevitable and therefore in some way acceptable or 'right'.

Here is a list of some of theories that you could well find useful in exploring A2 topics. It is not exhaustive but there again it's not prescriptive. There are other useful theories and some useful theories are not necessarily included. It is meant to be some kind way of guiding you into the intelligent use of theory for A2. If you want to do a proper job of learning about theory, then read the chapter on Theoretical Perspectives in *A2 Media Studies: The Essential Introduction*. For the moment perhaps a short quotation might persuade you to look a little more deeply:

> **Rather annoyingly, theories often suggest that something which had always seemed perfectly simple and straightforward is actually complex. As we shall argue later, the mass media have a particular knack of making things seem so obvious and so natural that it would be just plain daft to criticise or ask for explanations. In those areas, especially, it is important to have theories which never take anything for granted, theories which ask *how* and *why* we see things as obvious or natural.**
>
> **Bennett *et al.* (2005)**

You will perhaps recognise that we are back at the point we argued earlier in the chapter about everyone having some kind of opinion on the media. It is your grasp of and ability to apply theory that will separate your arguments and insights from the informed non-specialist. So you had better learn some if you have not done so already.

So here is our top ten media/cultural theories for you to brush up on:

1  Semiotics. If you don't know that semiotics is the study of signs by now, then sell this book and get a job.

2  Post-structuralism. Some interesting stuff here. This perspective takes semiotics and says that looking for meaning is pretty pointless because it is just about impossible to pin down meaning anyway. This position privileges hugely the consumers of media texts, audiences, as it is they who ultimately give a media text such meaning as it has. Rather makes the MED1 exam interesting doesn't it?

3  Postmodernism. An especially useful perspective which develops ideas from post-structuralism to argue that the divide between high and popular culture is irrelevant or even non-existent and there are no real unifying theories anyway because culture and society have become so fragmented.

4  Feminism. As a perspective for looking at media texts, feminists would see most media output as being the product of a patriarchal or male-dominated order aimed at disempowering women.

5  Queer theory. As its name suggests, queer theory is concerned with sexuality and identity. It sees gender as being constructed socially and to some degree through our association with the media. Consider some of the ways in which gender identity is represented in mainstream mass media output.

6  Marxism. It does seem a bit unfair to the world's greatest political thinker to reduce his views to a single bullet point. In media terms, Marxism is probably best seen through class war. A Marxist view of the media would be that mass media output functions as a means of keeping the proletariat, or working class, in its place to preserve the power of the capitalist ruling elite. Much media output is simply a diversion to deflect the workers from rising up against the power elite. You might like to check this idea out by reading a copy of *The Sun*.

7  Liberal pluralism. This perspective sees the mass media as being generally positive in its influence on society. It makes a play of individual choice and freedom which a free media does a lot to maintain in a democratic society. Liberal pluralism provides a handy place for liberal left wing intellectuals to sit on the fence.

8  Post-colonialism. With many of the global issues raised by the Bush/Blair invasion of Iraq, post-colonialism becomes an increasingly important perspective. Basically it identifies the role of the media in the Western domination of developing countries not least through the export of Western culture and social, economic and political systems to them.

9  Audience theory. You can read up on key audience theories in the section in the MED4 chapter.

10  Genre theory. You can similarly read up on genre theory there too.

A good activity you might undertake is to choose a text that you know reasonably well and to work through the list of perspectives to see how each might offer some insight into that text. Try to make a habit of this each time you look at a text, perhaps just choosing two or three perspectives that seem particularly appropriate and looking how they might be applied.

So, here's a brief recap on getting down to A2 study:

■  Don't forget that the specification is still very text centred. That means that you should always make texts your starting point and a constant reference point when exploring ideas, issues and debates.

■  You need to get a handle on wider contexts. These are the contexts of production and consumption as well as the wider social, political and economic contexts that shape the nature of media texts.

■  You need to learn to apply theory. If you are going to do really well, you need to apply it both appropriately and with confidence.

Finally, there is a section at the end of this book explaining to you how the exams that you take are set and marked. It is at the back of the book because if you don't have to read it, we didn't want it to get in the way. If you have time, however, give it a quick once over. There is some useful information in there that should help give you an insight into the exam process. It should also help you prepare for your exams by detailing some of the ground rules that examiners follow when they set exams. As you will see there are strict limits on what can and cannot be set. These are determined by what is laid down in the specification which you can access on the AQA website. If you are prepared to do a little bit of research into this, you should go into the exam room just a little bit better prepared for what is waiting for you.

# WHAT KIND OF STUDENT HAVE YOU BECOME?

If you have read our book *AS Media Studies: The Essential Revision Guide* for AQA, you will remember that we asked the question: 'What kind of student are you?' We divided students into two categories – active and passive. We explained that passive students were a real pain to teach because they were so heavily reliant on their teacher. They expected their teacher to do everything for them, including thinking. Ideally they would quite like their teacher to take the exam for them, providing of course that they managed to get a decent grade. We suggested that passive students were unlikely to do as well as they might expect at AS level because Media Studies is a discipline which seeks to reward students who do not rely on their teacher too heavily. It rewards the student who is prepared to think for themselves.

You will perhaps remember that these students who think for themselves are called active students. You may have got the impression that we like active students. Well you would be right. Active students are a pleasure to teach (although they can also be a pain) because they want to know. They have enquiring minds that enjoy finding out about things. In Media Studies this should translate into a desire to go and seek out media texts and to try applying some of the ideas that have been explored in class to them. Always bear in mind that you are very lucky to be able to study the media. Media texts are nearly always accessible and nearly always enjoyable. These are the raw materials of your programme of study. This is certainly not bad when you can spend an evening watching Ant and Dec or going to the cinema and you can call it homework.

With any luck if you started without the level of autonomy that you need to be an active student, you will have developed this to some degree by the time you are studying at A2. If you have not, then here is a serious suggestion: go and do something else. Without the ability to learn independently, you are wasting your time doing A2 Media Studies. The whole of the A2 assessment is geared towards your ability to get up and do things for yourself. Relying wholly on your teacher is a great way to do badly.

So why is this the case? Well as you will read in the next section, the transition from AS study to A2 study is marked by a shift from textual analysis to an application of wider contexts and theoretical perspectives. Put simply you are shifting away from textual study in its own right and looking at media texts in a broader way. You will have to look at the context in which media texts are produced and consumed. You will also have to look at some of the theoretical issues that underpin our study of the media at this level. This is a tall order.

So how do you start to tackle it? Well the key is developing your skills in independent research. Now fortunately this is one place where the A2 specification rallies round to help you. Ironically the key to your success in A2 exams lies in the coursework Unit MED5, also known as Independent Study. MED5 requires you to produce a 3,000 word essay on a topic of your choice. The basic limitations are that your study is text-based and contemporary. This means that you have to take as your starting point contemporary texts and use them to explore some wider issue in terms of contemporary media.

> There is nothing to stop you choosing a topic for MED5 that will overlap with at least one of your areas of study for MED4. Given that MED4 is made up of some pretty wide possibilities (see page 31) finding overlaps should not be too strenuous. Topics such as genre and representations are obviously central to most media texts so it makes sense to see how you might use your MED5 study topic as the basis for further exploration in MED4.
>
> NOTE

This is, of course, the same basic premise that should underpin the way you prepare for both of the external assessments in A2, MED4 and MED6. For each of these your starting point is texts: in the case of MED6 two unseen texts and in MED4 texts you have prepared in readiness for use as exemplification in the exam. In the next chapter we consider how you might go about this sometimes difficult task of seeking out contexts. For the moment however just get your head round the thought that if you want to do well at A2 you will need to be both independent in your choice of texts to explore and show the ability to explore the contexts that relate to these texts. The contexts are primarily production ones but can also relate to the consumption of texts.

ACTIVITY

*Imagine you are looking at the following possible topics for exploring for MED4. Identify some of the key media texts that you think it would be useful to consider. Then identify some of the contexts that you think might be important to understanding further the nature of these texts:*

*Reality television*

*Celebrity news stories*

*Digital technology and audiences*

The other big issue at A2 is theory. Media studies is a discipline full of theories. On one level this is great news because it allows you lots of opportunities for looking at theoretical perspectives. Any text you look at is likely to lend itself to a whole lot of different tools with which to prise it open. Marxist, feminist, or postmodernist theories are all likely to be applicable to the texts that you want to explore.

Of course, theories exist for no other purpose than to be shot down. Or at least so it might seem to you. Well perhaps you are not quite at the stage of your academic career when you feel equipped to challenge the major theorists. What you are in a position to do, however, is to question the validity of the theories that you come across. More simply you are in a position to question whether they are theories that are true on the basis of the texts that you have studied.

Don't forget you are studying Media Studies at a time when the discipline is in a state of flux. A lot of the theories and ideas that have been taken for granted for many years are being questioned, not least because they have become outdated in the face of the vast technological changes that have taken place in the way in which media texts are both produced and consumed.

NOTE

In his introduction to Web Studies (Gauntlett, D. (ed.) (2000) *Web Studies: Rewiring Media Studies for the Digital Age*, London: Hodder and Stoughton), David Gauntlett describes Media Studies research at the end of the twentieth century as having entered 'a middle aged, stodgy period'. He says it wasn't 'really sure what it could say about things any more'. He goes on to list some of the reasons why Media Studies has encountered these problems. You may well find it useful to check out what they are in Rayner, P., Wall, P., Kruger, S. (eds) (2004), *Media Studies: The Essential Resource*, Routledge.

So one thing that you should find in your research is that there are many opportunities to question the theories that form the basis for the Media Studies textbooks that you have been using. The hallmark of a really good active Media Studies student at A2 is this willingness to question what has gone before. That does not mean that you have a licence to go round rubbishing every theory you have encountered. There will be theoretical issues that you will feel remain useful and have an important application today. Equally you must realise that it is not an act of heresy to call into question some of the received wisdom that underpins media studies. You need to adopt a healthy scepticism about the ideas that you come across. Better still be prepared to test them out against your own experience of texts and contexts.

So with any luck you will have decided at AS to be an active student. At A2 you will now have to develop and extend your abilities as an active student. If you don't here is a dire warning of what might happen.

In the MED4 exam your examiner will probably find very little evidence of learning because you will rely too heavily on the materials the teachers have taught you. Your answers will appear as though they have been learned by rote and they will be very similar if not the same as everyone else in the class taking the exam. You will also find it difficult to respond to the actual question you are trying to answer in the exam. This is because you will not be flexible enough to adapt what you know to the question you are asked. Typically a passive student ignores the question and writes down what they have been told in class. That is a bad idea.

The MED5 Independent Study is your real chance to pursue some aspect of Media Studies that interests you. There is very little limitation on what you can explore as long as it is focused on text and is contemporary. You would have to be mad to ignore the opportunities it presents.

MED6: this exam is about thinking on your feet. It is a really stiff and demanding test of how good you are at applying what you have learned. If you go into the exam stuck at the same level of textual analysis as you were at AS you will do badly. In the MED6 exam, examiners are looking for a sophisticated response; the type of response that comes from being able to engage with the texts, contexts and theories in the way that only an active student can.

## ACTIVE OR PASSIVE – THE CHOICE IS YOURS

Finally, you have probably been nursed through A level by a caring teacher prepared to spend time with you when you needed extra help. The next stop is university where staff are very unlikely to spend extra time with you. It is sink or swim once you get there. Active students make pretty good swimmers.

# REVISING FOR A2 EXAMS

If you have got this far in your exam-taking career, you must know something about revising for exams. There again you may have just been lucky – these things happen. Assuming that your success to date is attributable to your own efforts in terms of study and revision, rather than luck, this a good point at which review what you are doing right and what you may be able to do better.

Look back over the exams that you took for AS level. You will remember that these consisted of MED1 Reading the Media and MED2 Textual Topics in Contemporary Media. You had to revise for both of these exams but it is likely that you felt it necessary to spend more time focused on revision for MED2 than for MED1. The reason for this is that MED2 requires you to bring rather more information to the exam than MED1, which was an unseen text that you were required to analyse.

Revision for AS exams consisted, therefore, of a combination of:

1   Learning and knowing how to apply concepts, specifically the Key Concepts

2   Finding examples of appropriate texts to exemplify your conceptual understanding

So you were looking at concepts and texts in parallel with one another so that in MED1 you felt confident in applying the concepts to an unseen text and in MED2 you were able to talk about the concepts and show your understanding of them through the use of texts that you had studied in preparation for the exam.

The good news is that the same basic principles should underpin your revision for the A2 exams. Indeed you will find that the exams that you take at A2 are disconcertingly similar to those you took at AS. Don't be fooled, however, into thinking that your revision strategy should be exactly the same. As you will have read in the introduction, although A2 may look the same, it makes significantly different demands on you. If you are smart, these different demands will become the prime focus of your revision.

Before we look at how to tackle these different demands, let's just remind you of some of the broad principles of revision in case you missed them first time round.

Number one job when revising is to get your notes sorted out. By this point in your A level study you should be good at taking notes. If you aren't, then it is time you learned. Of course being good at taking notes and keeping them organised are two different things. Notes that are not organised need to be organised sharpish if they are to be any good. So the first thing you need to do is to read through your notes to make sure that they make sense. If there are serious omissions then deal with this. You can do this either by swapping notes with other people in your class or finding the right resources and making the notes you have missed.

One skill you should have developed by now is the ability to make notes on media texts that have interested you and/or seem relevant to a particular area of study. Don't forget that some of the texts that you have studied for AS will also be relevant here. You may need to revisit and extend them to meet the demands of A2, but that may be easier than starting from scratch.

You will also need to get down useful notes from other sources. These will include textbooks and websites. One thing you must learn to be aware of here is the dangers of plagiarism. Your teacher will have warned you about this in relation to the Independent Study you have prepared for MED5. You will remember that if you quote from other sources then you are obliged to acknowledge the source that you have used. Clearly in coursework copying is much more of an issue than in an exam. However, bear in mind that in an exam it is always a good idea to acknowledge ideas that you have used from sources other than your own head. One very good reason for doing this is to let the examiner know that you have engaged with some of theories surrounding the topic you are writing about. Don't forget, therefore, in your notes to write down details of the sources you have used so that you will at least be able to mention the name of the author in the exam. In addition it may be that as part of your revision you may wish to go back to the original source to expand your notes.

NOTE

One skill you should have developed in your work on the Independent Study is the use of Harvard Referencing. You can read up on the detail on page 34 of *A2 Media Studies* if you do not know already. While it is both unnecessary and inappropriate to use the Harvard system in an exam, there is a lot to be said for adopting this notation for citing sources in your notes. It will certainly help you when you get to higher education and find yourself writing this sort of extended essay on a regular basis.

If you are going to do well at A2 level, good notes are absolutely essential. One reason for this is that you are going to collect a lot of background information that you may well need to help you in your exam answers. This is especially the case in the MED4 exam where a lot of preparation has to be made in advance if you are going to produce decent answers to the questions you tackle. The sort of background that is particularly important is contextual information about the texts that you are studying. In the section on wider contexts (page 4) we consider how best to research this information, but one thing that it is important to point our here is that much of it will come from sources that you will be less familiar with than the traditional textbooks and websites you have used previously for AS media studies.

As you see, we also suggest that you might go to some primary sources for information. Getting down notes from such sources is a different kind of challenge to researching material from books and websites. The skills in doing this are closely allied to those of a journalist or a media researcher collecting qualitative data. One thing you might do is consider asking the person you are interviewing if you can record the interview so that you can play it back later. You may find that your mobile has a facility to allow you to do this. Above all be sure you are properly prepared for the interview. In essence this means having an interview strategy planned usually in the form of questions that you intend to ask. Don't forget though that it is better to adopt a flexible approach to the interview rather than mechanistically asking your questions regardless of the response you are getting. As long as you stick to your basic strategy you should be prepared to pursue some of the more interesting issues and ideas raised by the interviewee.

Once you have established that you have all the notes you need, your second job is to organise them into a user-friendly manner. One way to do this is according to exam topic. Some of your notes may well go under a general heading. This might include for example some of the major theories that you feel you must know. Other sections might be centred around the MED4 topics that your intend to tackle. So you may have a section on genre. This might well include an overview of genre perhaps organised into sections such as:

- Genre and audiences
- Genre and producers
- Genre theory – the advantages
- Genre theory – the limitations

Much of the remainder of your notes in this section might be organised around the exemplification of the ideas contained in this section. You might also consider using the headings from the specification which as you will have read indicate the areas where questions may be asked. So a heading which deals with, say, the historical development of a genre would be especially useful in revising this potential exam topic area.

If you organise your notes along these lines they should both make sense and be easy to navigate. Spending time looking through notes and then finding they make no sense is a complete waste of time.

---

**ACTIVITY**

*In our AS Revision Guide (Barker, J. and Wall, P., AS Media Studies: (2006) The Essential Revision Guide, London: Routledge), we asked students to look at their notes and on the basis of that evidence to place themselves on a scale of 1 to 10 for adjectives that might best describe their approach to study. It might be a good idea to have a go at the same activity one year later. Here it is:*

1                                                                    10

| | |
|---|---|
| Active | Passive |
| Organised | Disorganised |
| Conscientious | Lackadaisical |
| Thorough | Erratic |

So how did you score this time? Of course the ideal is lots of low numbers. Realistically you would be pretty bad company if you really do live such a virtuous life. One the other hand you might be pretty bad company if you are scoring tens constantly. Most of you will be scoring an average somewhere in the middle.

You can use this as the basis for a SWOT analysis. SWOT stands for *S*trengths, *W*eaknesses, *O*pportunities and *T*hreats. As you may have guessed it is a bit of management-speak, but it can be useful to you as a Media Studies student. Knowing what your strengths and weaknesses are in terms of exam performance is going to be helpful to you in your preparation for the coming exams. You should also make yourself aware of what opportunities present themselves in the run up to your exam. For example the chance to visit a media organisation might be an opportunity to be grasped with both hands. Probably the biggest threat to your achievement is your own inability to knuckle down to the task ahead.

One place that you could very usefully start your SWOT analysis is with your AS exams and any mock exams that you have done for A2. First off for each of these it is worth standing back and making an appraisal along the following lines:

1  What did I achieve?

2  Was I surprised by my achievement?

3  Did I deserve this achievement?

4  What particular strengths did I take into the exam?

5  If I could do the exam again, what elements of my preparation would I improve on?

The answers to these questions should help you find a strategy for preparing for the A2 exams. Your aim should be to find a means of revising and preparing that will enable you to maximise your achievement. The last question is the one that needs most focus. As an A2 student you have already had the benefit of experiencing at least one set of Media Studies exams. Learn from the experience of doing these. Try to write yourself a list of three or four points where you think you might be better prepared this time. For example, you may think that you went into the MED2 exam a bit light on good textual examples. When you come to take MED4 make sure you get it right this time.

Another skill you should be on the way to developing is that of time management. At A2 the pressure is on, or at least it should be. Media Studies exams will just be one of the many demands on your time. The hours that you are able to devote to it are precious, so you must use them wisely.

One thing you will almost certainly know well in advance are the dates of your exams. You should have learned from your previous studies that taking a long run at your exams is likely to have much better impact on your results than a last minute sprint. This means that you need to plan your revision. Let's assume that you decide to start revising in earnest for your MED4 and MED6 exams a couple of months before they are due. That means that you have roughly 60 days to get yourself ready. How are you going to use these 60 days? Well of course you won't really have 60 days. There will be lots of other things to fill your time but you should try to give up between and hour and two hours a day for your A2 revision. So that means an average of about 90 hours for the two exams.

If you think about the two exams, MED4 and MED6, it should be apparent to you that there is rather more you can do in the way of revision for the former than the latter. The very nature of an unseen paper like MED6 tends to limit the amount of revision you can do. That does not of course mean that you don't do any. Far from it. What it does means is that the balance of time that you spend between the two exams should favour MED4 which demands more specific revision than MED6. You need therefore to arrive at a compromise which would give the following balance of hours:

**MED4 – 60 hours**          **MED6 – 30 hours**

This is not a hard and fast rule. It may be you want to shift the balance one way or another. That is for you to decide. You may even feel that the amount of hours suggested is far too many or far too few. Again that is for you to decide. The important issue here is that you spend at least some time revising and that the time you allocate is properly organised and spent wisely. Revision that is random is very difficult to sustain and usually quite unproductive.

**NOTE**

Don't forget about the therapeutic power of lists. Whenever possible write down a list of things you have to do as part of your revision programme. Your list can be either a short focused list of your revision topics or an epic list of things to do with your life more generally, including A2 Media Studies revision topics. Lists help you organise. More importantly they help you prioritise. One quality of being stressed is that you lose all sense of the amount of time a task might take or how difficult it might be. Every task seems like a mountain to climb.

Once you have a list try numbering the order you intend to do the items in. Group together tasks that you can undertake in the same location, e.g. the library. Try to build in some contrasts in the list: for example different activities or different topics so there is a variety in what you do. This helps stave off the boredom factor.

The therapy comes as you are able to feel the warm inner glow of crossing off items on the list until you finally get to the last one. Think then of the reward you have promised yourself for such virtuous dedication to your revision programme.

In the chapters on MED4 and MED6 we have a detailed look at how you should go about preparing for these exams. You may find it a useful thought to consider now what kind of organisational strategies you are going to adopt for your revision plan. Let's try to get you started.

The MED4 exam requires you to answer two questions from a total of four possible sections. Unless you are a super conscientious student you will have prepared just two topics for this paper. Given that you have a global figure of 60 hours to use for revision, logically you will split this time between the two topics, i.e. 30 hours each. Of course you may feel that one topic needs more attention than the other. Perhaps you have focused heavily on one topic, such as news, for your Independent Study and, therefore, feel more confident about it than the other topic. No problem here about adjusting the number of hours as long as you don't get blasé about it.

So how are you going to use these 30 hours for your topic? Well we can break it down into some of its constituent parts. These might include:

Core concepts: you can find these as bullet points which form the content of each topic area in the specification. There are usually between four and six bullet points to cover.

Texts: you need to look in detail at texts that you can use to exemplify the concepts you have identified above.

Contexts: this is potentially time consuming if you have not done the research as you go along. If you have then it is a matter of reading around the contexts in which the texts you have explored were produced. Of course, you then need to make links with these contexts, the texts and the concepts.

Theory: you need to feel confident that you know and can apply some of the key theories to all of the above.

So use these four headings as the basis of your revision checklist for each of the MED4 topics you intend to revise. You may want to allocate an equal amount of time to each. That is unlikely. Much more probable is that you will want to consider each in turn and prioritise them according to how much time you think each would benefit from.

So if you think theory is your weak area, then not only might this get a big slice of the 30 hours, it might also be the place you start your revision.

**ACTIVITY**

*Use the ideas and information above to help you draw up a revision plan for each of the MED4 topics. This plan should enable you to make the most effective use of the hours you intend to allocate to this unit. At this stage try to get a broad overview of what it is you need to confront in this unit. The fine tuning and detail can be added when we have sorted out your approach to MED6.*

MED6 revision poses a series of interesting challenges. Potentially MED6 is the most demanding area of assessment for the whole of the AQA Media Studies A level qualification. As you will read in the section on MED6, we are looking at more than textual analysis here. You may think that writing about an unseen text, as you did at AS, is in itself hard enough but in MED6 we are looking at two texts and we need to add some stuff about contexts and theories. So where can you start revising for that sort of exam?

Well it would be foolish to pretend it is easy. MED6 by its very nature is a voyage into the unknown. The only predictable element is that about six weeks before you take the exam, your teacher should be able to tell you if there is going to be a moving image text included. If there is a moving image text indicated, what they won't be able to tell you is whether there will be one such text or two. As you will see in the MED6 chapter it is quite common for AQA to set a comparison of a moving image text and a print text.

Preparing for MED6 is about getting yourself ready to respond on your feet to whatever is placed in front of you. The MED6 exam is probably the ultimate test of your ability to apply your conceptual understanding of the discipline of Media

Studies. So one thing that you need to make sure that your are up to speed on is the Key Concepts which played such a large part in your preparation for the AS exams. You should by now know exactly what they are, but just in case here they are again:

- Media Representations
- Media Language
- Media Institutions
- Media Values and Ideology
- Media Audiences

So one strategy for revision is to practise applying these KCs to any media text you come across in much the same way you did in preparing for the MED1 exam. You can do this formally by looking closely at a text and getting down notes under the Key Concept headings. Alternatively you can do it informally by mentally applying the concepts to texts that you encounter in your daily routine. Billboards on the way to school or college offer a rich opportunity for this type of activity.

The next step is to start looking for similarities in the texts you encounter. Obviously there will be similarities between texts in terms of genre and media form, but also look at issues of intertextuality where texts might relate to one another in slightly different ways; for example the relationship between a billboard advertisement and a television or magazine advertisement for the same product. Try to make some notes on how the two relate in terms of points of comparison. You might like to start at a fairly basic level by considering their similarities and differences. Have the key concepts handy to guide you on this. Issues of representation for example can be an interesting focus point – do the two texts represent the same thing in different ways or in very similar ways? Similarly get used to the idea of comparing the media language of different texts, for example how each one uses narrative to communicate to the audience. Any mention of audience should immediately get you thinking around that key concept. You may consider the different ways in which the texts address their audiences and what assumptions each text makes about its audience.

Being able to respond quickly to these kinds of cues is an important skill if you are going to do well in the MED6 exam. Remember though that this is baseline stuff, just a little way on from what you did in the AS MED1 exam. By now it should almost be second nature to reach for your analytical toolkit whenever a text or pair of texts captures your interest.

*Whenever you become interested in an individual text, start thinking about other texts that you might link it to. Put yourself in the position of the Principal Examiner for MED6 and try to identify texts that form interesting pairings. Do this across media forms as well. Think about how for example a moving image text might relate to a print text covering a similar topic or theme.*

As you will realise from your reading of the MED6 chapter, this kind of comparative textual analysis is very much a starting point in the exam, not an end point. As you will be aware two important issues are the linking in of wider contexts and theoretical perspectives. You should see the latter in revision terms as an extension of your application of the Key Concepts to the texts. By the time you have reached the revision stage you should have at least a nodding acquaintance with some of the key theoretical perspectives. Ideally you should be on first name terms with a good many of them. So get used to looking at individual texts and, better still, pairs of texts to see what theoretical perspective you think might be applied.

Getting your head round contexts for MED6 is much more demanding. There is clearly going to be some element of luck in the texts that turn up in the exam. You may or may not know something of the background to the texts that you are looking at. However, detailed historical knowledge about the background is not part of the mark scheme. What you have to learn to do is to read into the wider contexts via the texts themselves. Of course, some basic grasp of politics and recent history will help you here, so part of the way into revising wider contexts is through your own intellectual curiosity. Being aware of issues by doing simple things like reading the *Guardian*'s media supplement the 'Media Guardian' and taking an interest in 'serious' news will help you a lot here. Don't forget that you may have notes from other GCE subjects that might add to your broader knowledge of social and cultural contexts. History and Sociology are two of the subjects that might help. When you are confronted with a non-contemporary text or texts try to get some detail of the background. This is a skill you should have developed for both MED4 and MED5.

Try adding this contextual dimension to the text that you have looked at previously. Learn to move beyond the texts into the broader social and cultural issues that it raises. Focus for example on some of the ethical issues that certain texts might raise. Confessional television shows and newspaper 'exposés' of the private lives of celebrities all provide opportunities to rehearse a multitude of issues relating to media ethics.

Revising for MED6 is about learning to identify and exploit opportunities. Practise this both mentally and more formally by choosing pairs of texts and getting down an essay response in note form. You will be surprised how accomplished you can become at this.

## CREATING A PLAN – BEING PREPARED TO MODIFY IT

So you should have by now some idea of the task that is confronting you. The next thing to do is to create a plan. With any luck this is something you are used to doing after your experience of revision for AS Media Studies and your other AS exams. The best way to do it is by using a big wall planner or the calendar on your computer which has the delightfully irritating habit of reminding you on a hourly basis what you have to do.

Try to plan your revision to give yourself some variety. Look also at links between MED4 and MED6 revision. Certainly some of the theoretical stuff and the wider contexts may well overlap to save you time. Don't forget that watching a DVD or reading a magazine can count towards your revision providing you focus on their possible value as exemplars in an exam answer or preparation for unseen texts in MED6.

Remember too that your plan is a guide, not a binding contract. Don't ever let the plan become too much for you. Be prepared to trim it where necessary if you feel you are falling behind. Be prepared to prioritise paying attention to those areas that most need attention.

## HOW AND WHERE TO REVISE

You should by this stage have a clear sense of what is the most effective way for you to revise. If you have a system that works, then skip this section and get on with some revision. If you still find it hard to get on with revision then you may find some of the ideas below helpful.

You should really know by now what works best for you when it comes to the logistics of revision. If you don't then it is about time you found out. Here are some ideas that you might like to consider to help you. One thing you might like to do is go back to some advice we offered for your AS revision so that you can consider just where your time goes.

NOTE

## ACCOUNTING FOR YOUR TIME

It is important to remember that everyone is different. Consequently there are no hard and fast rules for how best to revise. What matters most is that you find out for yourself a method of revising that is going to be the most effective. You also need to find out a method of revising that makes optimum use of your precious time. Again this means getting organised. It is quite a salutary experience to make an analysis of how you spend your time over a period of a week, broken down in terms of the 168 available hours. A fairly rough breakdown will do. It can be realised in terms of activities like:

- Sleeping
- Working (as in paid employment)
- Study (in and out of class)
- Leisure activities
- Travelling

First, you need to think what has worked best so far. It is probably not a good idea to start trying out new revision strategies close to one of the most important exams you are likely to take. Think back to your most recent experience of exam revision. For most people this is likely to be the AS exam less than a year ago. You may also want to think back a little further to how you tackled your GCSE revision. One thing you probably noticed is that there is quite a significant difference in demand between GCSE and AS. You may also have noticed that AS calls for rather different skills.

Use the grid below to help you focus on how you went about AS revision, and what was good and what was not so good about your approach.

- Noise. Just how sensitive are you to noise as a source of distraction?

    Very sensitive                           Oblivious

- Hell is other people. How helpful do you find it to be supported by other people?

    Helpful                                  Really irritated by them

- Do you work best on your own or as part of a group of people revising together?

    Love groups                              Hate groups

■ Attention span. Different people have different attention spans. What is your optimum attention span? Do you start to flag after half an hour and need to go do something else for a short while to get your concentration and motivation back? Or can you keep going for a couple of hours especially with the promise of a reward at the end.

Can concentrate hours                    Ten minutes max?

■ Where is the best place to work to ensure you have access to everything that you need? Remember you may need to use a computer and textbooks as well as your notes.

Bedroom                                   Trafalgar Square?

■ Can you get anything useful done in short bursts for example, on short journeys or during breaks? It is a good idea to make sure you always have something useful to hand such as a textbook when opportunities for short bursts of revision arise.

Yes                                       No?

The answers to these questions should help you with your revision focus. Use them to optimise the conditions under which your revise. If you arrive at the conclusion that your best revision strategy is to work alone in your bedroom with a computer in complete silence for a maximum of an hour then try to create these ideal conditions. For example wait until the rest of the household has gone out or are in bed if quietness is a real imperative for you. Above all be prepared to be flexible. It may be that the only place you can find to work is with your laptop on the bus home with a set of earplugs in place. Life is never quite as you would like it to be.

# PART 1

# TEXTS AND CONTEXTS IN THE MEDIA (MED4)

# INTRODUCTION

You will no doubt immediately recognise the format of the MED 4 exam, Texts and Contexts in the Media, as being akin to the one you have already sat called MED2, Textual topics in Contemporary Media. Indeed, other than the actual topics covered, the two exams are almost identical. This poses an interesting problem of what is known in the exam business as progression. You are supposed to find exams at A2 more demanding than those you took at AS to show you have moved on or progressed to a higher level of engagement with and understanding of the subject. Given these identical formats, it is clear that the idea of progression must lie within either the content – the topics must be more difficult, the way the exam is marked – it must be harder to score high marks on this paper – or what you are being asked to do in response to the questions you have been set. Or maybe it is all three.

A look at the assessment objectives might be useful here. You will remember that assessment objectives define what it is you are being tested on. For MED4 there are three AOs that need to be addressed. These are:

**AO1: demonstrate knowledge and application of the key concepts employed within Media Studies and the evaluation of texts and ideas using the Key Concepts.**

**AO2: demonstrate knowledge and application of the wider contexts (historical, social, political, economic) relevant to Media Studies.**

**AO3: demonstrate knowledge, application and evaluation of major ideas, theories, debates and information relevant to the study of contemporary media.**

NOTE

Just to remind you of the key concepts:

Media Representations

Media Language plus Genre and Narrative

Media Institutions

Media Values and Ideology

Media Audiences

How do these measure up to the assessment objective demands that you met in preparing for MED2 exams? Well the one that clearly makes the difference is AO2 wider contexts. This is also the most heavily weighted of the assessment objectives which means it is the one for which the most marks are available in your MED4 essays. It means that you will have to focus hard on this objective when preparing for this unit.

NOTE

It is useful to see what the specification has to say about MED4. It suggests that there is strong continuity from previous i.e. AS modules and that textual analysis should be pursued with increasing confidence. However it has an important distinction from AS modules:

Whereas the emphasis in the AS modules was upon developing an under-standing of how texts work, here the major focus is also upon why texts are the way they are, and the immediate issues arising from them, the major ideas, theories and debates which inform them, and the wider historical, social, political and economic forces which have shaped them.

MED4 is a one hour and 30 minutes paper. It demands of you a response to two questions from a total of four sections. Each section has two alternative questions from which you have to choose one. The sections you can choose from are:

The production and manufacture of news

Representations

Genre

Audience

What might immediately strike you as odd is the selection of topics. Three of them are key concepts while the fourth, news, is obviously a topic area. As the first of the assessment objectives requires an application of the key concepts you can be forgiven for wondering why these key concepts are also a topic area for this exam.

Perhaps the underlying logic is that as the specification suggests, these key concepts are now located within a wider context and require more theoretical contextualising, so you are going to need to develop some of the basic ideas you used at AS into more a more complex response at A2. Let's see what this might mean in practice by looking at each of the topic areas in turn.

# THE PRODUCTION AND MANUFACTURE OF NEWS

The first thing that you might like to notice from the title of this topic is the emphasis it places on 'news' as an industrial process. We are being taken straight to the sharp end of the news process and being invited to consider not only how news is produced but also how it is 'manufactured'. This last word is not one that would please many journalists. Manufacture carries with it the connotations of something which is being made or created, fabricated even. Of course, most journalists would argue that news is in fact about 'truth'. Manufacture here is perhaps better seen as the idea of raw materials being refined into a finished product. In the case of news, these raw materials are events in the outside world which the production process of news gathering and presentation turns into a finished article in the form of a news bulletin, newspaper or online news information service.

It is a good idea to bear this emphasis in mind when you are doing your revision. You should be focusing on the production element of the news process rather than the reception element. Of course, there may well be some need to consider audiences for news, not least because of how the technology of production has impacted on the ways in which people consume news, but try to ensure that you target your research primarily at the production aspect of the process.

**NOTE**

Notice with this topic we are dealing with news in quite a broad sense of the topic. Unlike in MED2 when you may have covered British newspapers as a topic, we are not limited here to news in one specific medium. Indeed one way in which you can ensure that you revise effectively is to consider news in a pan media context, i.e. by looking at news across a range of different media. These should include:

- Television, including digital and satellite news channels
- Radio
- Print
- Internet
- Text messaging

As with all topic areas, it is important that you are guided by the bullet points which define the content of this topic in the specification. The first and probably most important of these relates to news values. Specifically it calls for you to look at:

## "News values, including institutional and cross media differences in news values"

Best then to know what is meant by news values before you even begin to think about the wider issues. 'News values' refers to the idea that some events are more important than others in terms of their coverage by the news media. News values will determine what is the lead, or most important, story on a news bulletin or in a newspaper. A really important story will be so significant that programmes on television and radio may well be interrupted to give audiences information about what has happened.

So news values is clearly concerned with deciding the priority given to news stories in any given bulletin or edition of a newspaper. You can obviously do some research into what the news media prioritise simply by looking at some bulletins or newspapers and seeing what order they put stories in. Of course what is interesting is to figure out some of the general principles that are used for determining what stories get priority and which don't. Unfortunately most candidates at this point have recourse to Galtung and Ruge (Galtung, J. and Ruge, M.H. (1965) 'The structure of foreign news: the presentation of the Congo, Cuba and Cyrpus crises in four Norwegian newspapers', *Journal of Peace Research*, 2: 53–91), a couple of Norwegian theorists researching forty years ago. While the work was relevant then and within the context of Norwegian news media, its value in the twenty-first-century UK is perhaps a little more doubtful. A more useful source of theory in terms of news values is provided by Tony Harcup and D. O'Neill (Rayner, P., Wall, P. and Kruger, S. (2004) *Media Studies: The Essential Resource*, London: Routledge). They analysed 1,000 stories and came up with some alternative categories by which they argued the news media gave priority to certain stories. You might find these categories handy when you look at the nature of news values.

---

**HARCUP'S LIST FROM *MEDIA STUDIES: THE ESSENTIAL RESOURCE***

1   *The power elite*: stories concerning powerful individuals, organisations or institutions.
2   *Celebrity*: stories concerning people who are already famous.
3   *Entertainment*: stories concerning sex, show business, human interest, animals, an unfolding drama, or offering opportunities for humorous treatment, entertaining photographs or witty headlines.
4   *Surprise*: stories that have an element of surprise and/or contrast.
5   *Bad news*: stories with particularly negative overtones, such as conflict or tragedy.
6   *Good news*: stories with particularly positive overtones, such as rescues and cures.
7   *Magnitude*: stories that are perceived as sufficiently significant either in the numbers of people involved or in potential impact.
8   *Relevance*: stories about issues, groups and nations perceived to be relevant to the audience.
9   *Follow-ups*: stories about subjects already in the news.
10  *Newspaper agenda*: stories which set or fit the news organisation's own agenda.

This is a useful point to clarify the relationship between theory and practice, an issue that sometimes confuses students. Theories, such as those about news values, seek to explain the way in which the media works and behaves. The news editor on a newspaper or on a television news bulletin will decide on the stories that will be covered largely using his or her professional experience and a knowledge of the institutional expectations of the media organisation for which they work. What they don't do is have a copy of a media textbook outlining theories of news values and decide how to apply this.

NOTE

Understanding this issue is central to how you apply theory in the exam. Theories seek to explain the behaviour of people who work in the news media; they don't determine it.

It would be a good idea in preparing for the exam to look in detail at a news bulletin or a newspaper and see how well you feel you can match the above list of factors to the actual evidence in one edition of a bulletin or newspaper. You might also try to explain or account for any discrepancies between the theory and the practice here.

Such an exercise might lead you on nicely to the other aspect of this point on news values – institutional and cross media differences in news values. Do not for one minute think that this is a simple and straightforward comparison of how television news is different from print news or how BBC news is different from ITV. Both of these are obviously important areas that you need to explore and seek out textual examples and evidence. Explaining such differences is, however, a complex business based on a whole range of factors, many of which emerge in the other points you have to cover. You might like to consider for example how such factors as speed of delivery, technology, audience appeal, scheduling and regulation might determine the decisions that inform how different stories are prioritised in different media.

Of course, that is not to say that a good starting point for your revision might be to collect at least one example in which you have studied how different news media have prioritised the news over a 24-hour period. You might for example start by comparing the early evening news bulletins of the two main terrestrial channels, BBC and ITV. This could then be broadened into investigating the coverage of Sky News, and some of the bulletins put out by the digital channels such as BBC3 as well as Channel 4, Five and BBC2. Think about how radio covers news too. Note that radio does not have the same need for video footage (sometimes called visual imperative) as television news and this may have some bearing on the priorities given to different news stories in this medium.

The following morning's national newspapers will probably provide you with the best point of comparison with the television and radio bulletins you have considered.

NOTE

Don't forget there is a limit to what you will be able to remember for the exam. Don' get carried away. If you find this topic fascinating then come back to it when you are on your media degree course. Try to use your research to pull out some of the key features you have identified and select examples from the texts you have looked at to expand on these. It would be a good idea to draw up a grid that would allow you to make fairly straightforward comparisons of coverage across the media by identifying differences of priority in the main stories, rather than working your way through the running order of a whole bulletin or the pages of an entire edition.

Such research can provide you with some pretty useful exemplification to use in any essay that comes up on news values and prioritising news. Of course, as we have suggested above, it is important that you try to get at the 'why' factor in all this. Why is it that some news media have a different notion of what constitutes important news from that of others? It is a good idea to try to find some answers to this question before you go into the exam room. You might like to think about such basic points as:

- The nature of the medium
- The nature of the audiences
- Speed of delivery

This list should at least get you started thinking about some of the key issues that impinge on news selection and coverage.

One interesting dimension that we have not touched upon is to consider the way in which the increase in potential news outlets has made available to audiences niche channels that deliver news from an overtly biased perspective, although some would argue that this is also true of much mainstream output. A good example of this is the Qatar-based channel Al Jazeera which puts out news from a radical Islamic viewpoint. It is the only channel that broadcasts messages from militant Islamic figures such as Osama Bin Laden. One of the implications of the digital and new media revolutions is that we are all potential news broadcasters, determining our own news values and prioritising the stories we think are most important. These ideas are explored further below when we look at weblogs and podcasting.

## NEWS SOURCES

You really do have to learn about where news comes from. This is one area of the specification where you need to obtain and retain information if you are going to tackle a question on this topic. That is not to say that we are looking at a wholly factually based response here. The sources of news are obviously going to have a vitally important bearing on the actual nature of it.

One of the important illusions that the news media seems to enjoy perpetrating is the idea that news is unexpected. The presentation of news particularly on television creates an impression for the audience that journalists chance upon a lot of information and then present it as part of the bulletin. The amount of news that is unexpected is quite minimal. We suggested earlier that the title of this topic suggested some kind of industrial process. As with any industry, the news media needs to have a good supply of raw materials that are readily available to it on a daily basis. The raw materials of the news industry are such sources as:

- Parliament
- The government
- The courts
- Press releases
- The royal family
- Sporting events

All of these sources provide regular information that can be predicted in advance so that reporters and camera crews can be ready in place to cover the news aspects of these stories. So for example if the Queen opens a new hospital, this event will have been planned many months in advance and the media will have a good deal of opportunity to get everything in place to cover the story.

ACTIVITY

*Check through a bulletin on TV and/or radio and check out how many stories the news editor would have known about in advance. For each, identify the source of the story. Keep the results of your research as they will almost certainly come in useful in the exam.*

Many stories come from various sources within the government. Some of these are simply factual information that the government wants people in the country to know. Other stories are part of what is known as 'spin'. Spin is an important concept that you need to understand. Spin is taking a story and telling it from a particular point of view, inevitably one that will show the government in a positive light. You should try to find some examples of spin from the government or other sources. These will provide you with important wider contexts if you tackle a question on news sources and their significance. There is, of course, an important ethical issue here, one that concerns the important concept of ideology. Should the government be using the media to get across a particular point of view that fits in with its own specific interests? Certainly there are issues concerning the ways in which the independence of the news providers such as the BBC can be compromised that you may want to explore here. Also the role of public relations specialists such as Max Clifford who represent celebrities to ensure they get media exposure is another area you might like to look at.

## BALANCE AND BIAS

Most of the news media that is broadcast on television and radio is under an imperative to report in an objective and unbiased manner. Of course, that begs a huge question as to what we mean by these terms. Many would argue that the very nature of news which can be so heavily reliant on those establishment sources identified above is inevitably biased to represent the establishment point of view. No such demand for objectivity is made of the print media.

A newspaper such as the *Daily Mail* makes no secret of its Conservative bias and prints stories which are selected to reflect this bias. Historically the British press has always had a right wing bias and generally shown support for the Conservative Party in preference to the Labour Party. Part of the success of the Blair New Labour government has been to maintain the support through three elections of Rupert Murdoch's *Sun* newspaper, which claims to have such an impact on the outcome of British general elections.

NOTE

Balance and bias are particularly important in the coverage of political stories. British politics is dominated by the Labour and Conservative parties. The essence of 'balance' can be seen in some ways to represent the view of both equally. If one side is represented more favourably than the other, then the news media can be accused of bias. So balance and bias are focused around the idea of giving equal and fair coverage to both sides in any particular conflict. For example in the case of industrial action, then the viewpoints of both strikers and the employers should be represented equally and without the journalist taking one side or another.

How far this is possible particularly when journalists may be working to tight deadlines is an interesting question. However, there is a lot of evidence to suggest that broadcast news is considered by many people to be far more reliable than that which they read in the print media.

Within a wider contexts framework there are obviously a lot of issues that you may want to explore on this topic. One that is central to any discussion of news objectivity is that of freedom of the press. It has often been argued that a free press, by which we mean mostly newspapers, is essential to a healthy democracy. The news media and the print media often style themselves as protectors of democratic freedoms by acting as guardians of our individual rights. They would argue that by being free to expose the wrong doing of individuals, corporations and governments they are protecting society. A similar argument might well be offered by the broadcast media, part of whose job is to present facts about events to the population as a whole. In doing so they are also instrumental in maintaining a healthy democracy by ensuring people stay informed about important issues. How far the press and broadcast media can be said to do this is a matter of some debate. However, the important issue is their right to do so, free of interference from governments. That, of course, raises another issue: how far does this right extend? What limits should be placed on the news media in their search for 'the truth'. For many years, BBC News ran on the basis that any story had to be verified through two different sources. This clearly limited the BBC in seeking to find exclusive stories so valued by other news media in getting one over the competition. This need to create a product that will be appealing to an audience is a key factor also in what news media include. This has lead to accusations of the news being dumbed down and becoming fixated with reporting the antics of celebrities in its desire to maintain and increase its audience particularly in the face of competition from new media. Television media are often accused of tabloidisation in that they seek to imitate the popular press by focusing on gossip and scandal at the expense of more serious news stories.

This should suggest to you a good range of activities that you might pursue in considering some of these important issues in preparation for your MED4 exam. Certainly looking in close detail at a new bulletin on one of the terrestrial channels from the perspective of balance and bias should give you some interesting material for an essay on this topic and other similar, related topics. You might like to consider the extent to which you feel that stories within the bulletin seek to produce a sense of balance as well as the idea of balance within each individual story itself. Similarly you might also like to consider whether other viewpoints are represented in the news. For example you might want to consider a news bulletin from a feminist perspective or a post-colonialist one and explore the extent to which you feel minority groups are represented and how accurately. Similarly a survey of the national newspapers on one day would give you a perspective on whether collectively, rather than individually, they represent a balanced range of opinion. A liberal pluralist perspective would suggest that they do and that this is an indication of the healthy state of our democracy. A Marxist would obviously take a much more jaundiced view and see the press as another instrument of the power elite for maintaining their control over the proletariat.

*It is often a god idea to focus on one particular aspect of news coverage to enable you to arrive at some judgements about the nature and function of news. You might for example like to start collecting information and ideas about how police and crime stories are covered. This is an interesting field not least because there is usually quite a lot of this material in the news. As you are doing so, think about the relationship that the police have with the news media. You will see that police stories are a good source of material for all news media, not least because the fear of crime is common to most members of the audience. The police obviously use the media for helping solve crimes by getting information to the public, for example about people wanted for criminal activity. So the relationship most of the time is mutually beneficial. Do the media, however, cover stories of police incompetence and corruption? If so, how? How far do the police use the media for their own public relations purposes, for example when they have solved a major crime and the perpetrators are behind bars? How do the television news media get to be in a position for example to film 'surprise' dawn raids on alleged criminals' homes? Try to collect some examples from bulletins and newspapers to answer these questions and see what conclusions you can draw.*

## TECHNOLOGY

This has become a huge topic in news production especially since the arrival of digitalisation. It is an area of this topic that requires you to do quite a lot of research but you should be able to use much of this information even if the question of technology does not come up directly as it is important background to many of the changes in news production, presentation and consumption generally. Part of the problem with technological change is to know just how recent change has to be for consideration. Much of the technological change in print media took place some 30 years ago when newspaper production moved from hot metal technology to the more modern print technology we have today. Although this fundamentally changed working practices in the newspaper industry and shaped the nature of newspapers today, it is anything but a recent change and as such is not really central to any issues of technological change in the specification. The advent, however, of newspaper websites is significantly more recent and this is an issue that you will have to tackle in terms of news technology. Such a topic clearly invites you to undertake some kind of comparison. There is the opportunity to make comparisons between Internet sites of established titles, such as Guardian unlimited and a hard copy of the *Guardian* itself, or the Online Sun and a copy of the *Sun*. In addition it is worth bearing in mind that a useful comparison can be made between different newspapers' websites to determine how news organisations have decided to use new media technologies to complement their print titles. For example a comparison of the Guardian Unlimited site and Online Sun will show that the *Guardian* site, as you might expect, seeks to offer a much more comprehensive database of news information than does that of the *Sun*. You will notice for example that the *Sun* sees its page 3 feature as a valuable online resource that readers may like to access.

It is interesting to note also that the Sun website enjoys teasing readers with alluring headlines plus the opening two or three paragraphs of a story to tempt the reader to go buy a copy of the actual newspaper to find out the full information on a story.

This difference in approach seems quite fundamental to the way in which News International and the Guardian Media Group see the role of new media technology. Interestingly one facility offered by the *Guardian* is the opportunity to subscribe to the full edition of the newspaper delivered online. It is possible therefore to access a current edition of the newspaper from anywhere in the world that has Internet access and to print it as hard copy.

Don't forget that one of the implications of this important idea of the global village is its potential to further reinforce the idea of the local community and local identity. Most local newspapers now have their own websites, so that it is possible to get news of your own local community regardless of how far away you have travelled. News with its use of technology is clearly a good example of that postmodern phenomenon the compression of time and space.

Technology has important implications for the way in which news is both produced and consumed. Traditionally control of the news media has been in the power of rich and powerful entrepreneurs who were able to afford the means of producing and distributing news. This is still very much the case with organisations like Rupert Murdoch's News International which has influential cross media interests both in this country and abroad. However, Internet technology has also meant that individuals are able to distribute their own news through such means as weblogs and podcasting. It is a good idea to have a look at some examples of these to give you some idea of how the Internet has enabled people to produce their own news information services for a great variety of different reasons including an opportunity to represent directly to the world their own individual viewpoint without it being mediated, and some would argue misrepresented, by the professional news media.

An ancillary issue to this idea of the web having empowered people to communicate their views and ideas directly is that of interactivity. The digital 'revolution' has enabled both increased participation by audiences in news media and increased opportunities for people to select their own news rather than the selection process being cast in stone by the producers of news. Increasingly news bulletins on both television and radio offer opportunities for audiences to offer feedback and contributions to the news that is broadcast. Email and text messaging are just two ways in which audiences are encouraged to comment on news items or even to contribute their own. Consider also the use of footage shot by viewers on mobile phones and digital cameras. Often newsreaders appeal directly for this so-called 'user-generated material' thus creating a dynamic and seemingly empowering relationship between the newsroom and the audiences as they work in partnership to bring the latest bulletin.

In terms of the influence of technology on news agendas, while the news bulletin remains important, audiences are also able to set up their own news information pages on websites in such a way that they can select the type of news that they wish to receive. For example the home page of Yahoo! UK can be set up to select specific categories of news, for example sports news and showbiz news. It is worth exploring some of the possibilities on the web for setting up specific news pages to deliver particular categories of news.

A good example of audiences contributing to news production occurred at the time of the London tube bombings in July 2005. Footage of the immediate aftermath of the incidents was shot by survivors using the cameras on their mobile phones as they were evacuated past scenes of carnage from the carriages of the tube trains. This provided dramatic at-the-scene footage for the news bulletins broadcast later in the day. The events of 7th July gave rise to the phenomenon of the 'citizen journalist', a name coined to describe members of the public who provide footage for television news bulletins.

NOTE

Organisations such as the BBC and Sky have invested significant sums of money on the process of digitalisation. This has had an important effect on the way in which news is now delivered. The breaking down of the screen into individual frames is clearly evident on for example the Sky Sports News channel, as is the use of ticker tape information running along the bottom of the screen. The influence of computer technology is evident here. The rolling news channels not only offer 24-hour news coverage but also allow some limited degree of interactivity on the part of the audience who are able to select specific news reports to view on demand. Audiences are no longer limited to hourly news bulletins to get the information that they seek. At the same time news constantly presents itself as a commodity that we cannot do without or perhaps even escape from.

**ACTIVITY**

*Spend some time listening to BBC Radio's Five Live programmes. It is a good idea to dip in and out of the programmes over the course of a day or two. How is the flow of news on these stations organised? How do they fill the air time on this station?*

Of course, such innovation has implications for both the content and style of news. With the need to produce news that will fill our screens for 24 hours a day, there is inevitably a lot of repetition of news items on a rolling basis. Similarly news organisations find ongoing stories particularly attractive. The ability to go to a reporter on the scene for an update not only fills screen time, but is also a means of hooking audiences into an ongoing news narrative. In consequence there is a danger that stories that lend themselves to this type of coverage get pushed high up in the news agenda.

As you can see technology has a wide and varied influence on the nature of news, particularly in terms of how audiences now consume news. It is important to remember though that the chief concern of this topic is with the production of news. Here too technology has played an important role. If you have the opportunity to look back to some of the old Pathé newsreel footage which was shown in cinemas after the Second World War – it becomes clear that today's modern television news coverage enjoys significant advantages. Lightweight camera equipment, the use of the video phone and satellite links are just some of the ways in which reporters are able to send back reports from distant and inaccessible parts of the world.

Technology has also influenced the way in which we now see a lot of news on our television screens. The traditional television studio with its presenters sat behind desks, shuffling papers has largely been replaced with the virtual studio in which news readers walk round the studio encompassed by the actuality that is the bulletin they are presenting. It is as though they are at the virtual epicentre of the news universe with information being beamed to them by the minute ready to be disseminated to the viewing public. News in this way clearly revels in its own image as being hi tech and cutting edge. The whole design of the studio suggests authority and efficiency in delivering the events of the world into our living rooms.

## POLITICAL, SOCIAL AND ECONOMIC VALUES

As you will have seen the news media is a powerful tool not only for informing people about the world at large but also for shaping their attitudes towards that world. It should be obvious to you that the news media are a key influence not only on what we see of the world but also the way in which we interpret what we see. It is perhaps no surprise that in this country successive governments have ended up at some point at loggerheads with the BBC. The most recent example of this surrounds the Hutton Report (the inquiry led by Lord Hutton into a BBC report that the government had 'sexed up' its dossier on Iraq's weapons prior to the Iraq war). The BBC news has, however, developed over the years a reputation for impartiality and for reporting the world objectively and honestly, whatever we mean by those words.

So the political significance of the news media cannot be underestimated. As we have seen the British national press is generally anything but impartial and many of the popular titles promote a generally right wing, xenophobic, anti-European agenda. It would not be unrealistic to argue that this influence has impacted on the British political scene to such a degree that the Labour Party which traditionally represented a left wing perspective has been forced to move much further to the centre right of British politics in order to become electable. Certainly a Marxist view would be that the popular press is at best a distraction to class war and at worst an enemy of the proletariat. Certainly there are many who would express concern over the concentration of so much of the new media into the hands of a few powerful figures. A more liberal view, however, would be to suggest that the very diversity of the British news media is sufficient to ensure an overview which is fair and impartial in reporting the important events that can be considered as news.

Let's have a look at some of the questions that candidates have been asked to answer in previous exam series.

In June 2004 the two questions set were:

a  **Newspaper figures are on a downward trend. To what extent are newspaper websites part of this decline?**

b  **'News is always unexpected.' How far is this true?**

AQA June 2004

The first thing to notice about any pair of questions is the extent to which it restricts you. Notice that question (a) does not encourage you to talk about broadcast news. It focuses on print and new media news output exclusively. If you have prepared material extensively on other news media then it is not a wise idea to tackle this question. The second question (b) on the other hand invites you to deal with the topic of news in the broadest terms. You are invited to focus on the concept of news rather than specific news media outputs, thus leaving you relatively unrestricted in terms of the examples you draw upon in responding to this question.

Notice too that question (a) invites you to engage with a specific proposition. It asks you to explore the link between the decline in mass circulation and the advent of newspaper websites. A series of paths should immediately suggest themselves to you.

- To what extent is it true that circulation figures are on the decline? If you have some figures to support this information, this will show that you have a grasp of the question. You might also consider if this downward trend is specific to particular types of newspaper, the popular press for example. Remember that the newspaper market is quite fragmented and it may be dangerous to make generalisations.

- How might websites be part of this decline? Here you need to consider the relationship in both general terms and specific terms between newspapers and their websites. You need to consider a number of titles and explain how the hard copy of the newspaper and the website differ and how they complement each other. In general terms, some survey of how the two are likely to be accessed and used is probably an important key to this question. Remember that access to the web is far from universal, so the type of access you have to new media technology is unlikely to be shared by the population as a whole. Of course there is a future dimension that may be worthy of mention. As wi-fi hotspots and mobile phone technology become more prevalent, do these sound the death knell of newspapers as hard copy? Is the future a daily paper delivered on screen with the option to print for those who need it? A number of newspaper websites are now including newsreel footage in direct competition with broadcast media.

- What other factors might be at play in this so-called downward trend in circulation? If people have stopped buying newspapers it does not necessarily imply that they have deserted these for the website equivalent. It may be that they are simply doing something else with their time: for example, playing computer games, listening to the radio, downloading music or reading a free copy of *Metro* on their journey to work. They may even simply rely on their mobile phone for information.

- The idea of trend is important. What it means is that there is a general decline. Newspaper circulation on a daily basis may well go up as well as down. You need to identify some of the factors that can contribute to this. Obviously big, dramatic news stories will be a factor. The London bombings and 9/11 are two obvious examples. However, promotions of various sorts, free DVDs, bingo games, serialisations of biographies of celebrities can all influence circulation on a short term basis.

---

*Using the bullet points above, produce a plan for this essay using 6–8 key headings. For each heading, identify examples that you might use to support what you are saying.*

**ACTIVITY**

---

At first sight, question (b) is a much broader conceptually based question dealing, as it does, with the broad and potentially abstract concept of news. However, an abstract answer is not going to be all that appropriate here. Look carefully and you should see that the question is focused on the sources of news. Clearly if you know anything at all about the production and manufacture of news you will realise that the assertion that news is always unexpected is absurd. The majority of news sources are both predictable and pre-planned. Some events such as disasters, accidents and acts of terrorism are not expected, but these make up a relatively small amount of the news that is distributed each day. So what you might need to tackle this question is as follows:

- Some detail of the sources of news that are predictable and pre-planned. For example, government sources, the courts, press releases, follow-ups of previous news stories

- Examples of two types of news story: the expected and the unexpected

- Some comparison of how these two types of news story are covered

- The ideological implications for the nature of news that so much of the news agenda is fixed by powerful institutions

- The role of PR and spin in determining news agendas

- The nature of news presentation that seeks to give the illusion that news is in some way 'discovered' or unearthed by journalists rather than being handed on a plate to the news media

It might be a good idea in an essay of this type to give a brief overview of how news is processed into the form that it finally takes when it appears in a bulletin, in a newspaper or online. The important role of news editor is certainly worthy of mention in terms of talking about how news agendas are set.

Examples are clearly important here and it is necessary for you to have some good examples prepared well in advance of the exam. Obviously it is unlikely that this question exactly as it appears here will be set again, but good examples of news from different sources is adaptable to a range of questions that ask you to explore the nature of news agendas. A question of this type requires you to support your knowledge of news sources and agendas with a judicious use of stories that will help clarify and explain the points you are making.

Let's have a look at some of the challenges set for this topic in past MED4 papers. Here are the two alternatives from the January 2005 paper:

a   **Discuss the impact of recent changes in the production and presentation of news.**

b   **Which factors cause the news agenda to differ from day to day?**

**AQA January 2005**

The first thing to notice is that these are two very different questions. Although there may be some overlap between them, they are asking for two very different things. So don't think a one-size-fits-all response can be slotted into either question. You are being asked for a specific response here. The first question is about changes in news production and manufacture whereas the second is asking you about how news agendas are set. We can see the fundamental differences between the two when we look at them one by one.

Question (a) is a 'discuss' question although the word is not used. It also focuses on the 'impact' of changes. This should signal to you immediately that simply writing down a list of changes in technology and presentation style is not going to be enough to answer this question. It will, however, get you started. The other word that needs attention is 'recent'. To some extent it is up to you to define what is meant by recent. However, realistically we are talking about the past few years as opposed to back in the 1980s when the transition from hot metal newspaper production would have been an issue.

Notice also that no specific media form is mentioned. The words 'production' and 'presentation' can be as easily applied to print as they can to television. You might even consider bringing radio as a potential medium into your answer. It would, however, be fair to say that television news probably lends itself best of all the media to exploring issues of production and presentation. Of course it would be possible to look at a combination of different media, but there is a danger that this might lead you to produce too diluted a response.

Assuming you have decided to base your answer around the changes in television, you need to start by making a list of key items that you feel need to be explored. Your list of production issues might contain the following:

Internet technology

Computer screens

Mobile phones

Weblogs

The global electronic village

24-hour rolling news

Audience participation/interactivity

Digitalisation

Remember we cautioned you that just producing a list was inappropriate. The focus of the question is the impact of these changes. How have these changes influenced what appears on our screens? Bear in mind that this links in closely with the other half of the question, the issue of presentation of news. Remember too that you also need to consider how you might use evidence to exemplify the points you are making.

For each of the headings, you need to suggest the impact it has made. In your plan this information can be written next to the heading. So you might end up with a list of points as follows:

**Internet: facilitated journalists' research. Competition with TV broadcasts. Empowered audiences to select type of news they want. See Weblogs**

**Computer screens: TV multi screening, ticker tape, impact on digital teletext services (presentational device)**

**Mobile phones: bespoke news service delivered direct to audience – link to BBC 24-hour news multi screen (presentational device)**

**Weblogs: audience empowerment/participation. Democratisation of news reporting**

**Global village: delivery of news from remote parts of the world using devices such as video phones. Fast delivery of 'breaking news'. Natural disasters good examples**

**Rolling news: pressure on television news producers to fill screen time 24 hours a day. Breaking stories and access to world news become increasingly important. Dedicated sports news coverage via Sky Sports**

**Audience participation: use of mobile phone, email and digital interactivity to involved audiences in news issues, for example through voting or sending in views on specific issues. Presentational device – how representative are the views?**

**Digitalisation: allows dedicated news channels, audience interaction, multi screening, choice of news coverage**

In terms of presentation, there are several additional items that are covered through your consideration of changes in production. These might include:

- The creation of virtual studios to create a news environment.

- Allied to this the use of computer graphics to create virtual effects in the studio and on screen.

- The style of presenters – a key item. The move from formal authority of the presenter behind a desk to the more informal approach favoured say by ITV

News and Channel Five. Remember to explore reasons for this – attention spans, news as entertainment, etc.

- Reporting styles, use of videophones, etc.

- Multi-screening techniques such as ticker tape and infobars.

You will almost certainly find it useful to have some detailed textual evidence to hand to exemplify some of these points. Detailed analysis of at least one bulletin would help but you should also have collected examples of variations between different news providers on different channels. You might like to check out the analysis of a news bulletin in *A2 Media Studies: The Essential Introduction* (page 179) if you are uncertain how to get started.

Question (b), the alternative question, makes rather different demands. You should notice immediately that the focus of this question is news values and news sources. If you feel confident that you have a good grasp of these two core concepts within this topic, then this is the question for you. Note that the question asks you to consider which factors. As with question (a) a list is not enough. To get into the higher mark bands you are going to have to explain why these factors influence the daily news agenda. Another word of caution – this is not the opportunity you have been waiting for to rehearse Galtung and Ruge. Some of what they say may, of course, be relevant, but as we have pointed out earlier a lot of this is dated theory. As with question (a) you are not limited here to one specific media form. The news agenda applies as much to print as it does to television, radio and the Internet. You may well feel that this question lends itself much more to a pan media take than question (a). Equally you might argue that by looking tightly at one medium, you can better demonstrate your theoretical grasp. The choice is very much yours.

A good place to start is by defining what we mean by the news agenda. Agenda setting is an important issue in news reporting. Start by explaining how you think news agendas are set. What are the factors that not only influence the inclusion of items into the news but also how these are prioritised to arrive at a running order, say for television news bulletins? Of course this might be a good opportunity to make some pan-media comparisons. Television news for example is far more driven by the need for visual imperatives, actuality to include in bulletins, than is radio, which relies more on actuality provided through sound imperatives or newspapers which rely on still photographs.

You might like to consider how very often the popular press is driven by other factors than the supposed 'importance' of specific news stories. Often popular newspapers will be involved in a 'feeding frenzy' in terms of an ongoing news story. Moral panics for example or a particular celebrity who has fallen foul of the media are such possibilities. Such stories may be wholly ignored by radio and television news. The importance of prevailing issues and the individual ideological agendas of the popular press cannot be underestimated in the coverage of news stories and the consequent agenda setting.

You need to give a brief run down of potential sources for news stories at some point. Avoid slavishly writing lists of such sources. Perhaps the best way to make a differentiation between different sources is through the idea of expected and unexpected news. You can highlight the fact that a high proportion of news is in fact completely predictable and that news organisations often determine the day's agenda at an early morning news conference. This would be a good opportunity to talk about some of the ways that the government and other institutions are able to dominate the news agenda.

> **NOTE**
>
> Don't forget the idea of ownership and control is an important issue here. The coverage of some stories might well have been influenced by the interests of the proprietor of a popular newspaper for example. There is often criticism of the BBC in titles owned by News International, such as the *Sun* and *The Times*, not least because of Rupert Murdoch's other major media interest, Sky Television.

Of course, there is also the issue of wider contexts to consider. There is a real danger that your response to this question might become very narrow. You can avoid this in questions of this type by linking in to the wider backdrop. Here it would be appropriate to look at the role of news organisations within Western democracies such as in the United Kingdom. The role of the news media to protect our democratic interests is well established. One way in which news does this is through investigative journalism, revealing information that governments and other powerful organisations would prefer us not to know. You would do well to collect examples of such stories to use in an essay like this.

Theoretical perspectives similarly need some focus here. Certainly perspectives such as Marxism and feminism would see the news media as an instrument of the rich and powerful (and usually male) establishment. However, a pluralist view would see the great diversity of news media as the sign of a healthy democracy in which a spectrum of views is available to us, the audience. They would argue that news can come from a whole range of sources, not just one.

This is a good example of a question where you should be able to see that while on the surface there may be a very simple rehearsed answer, the nature of the MED4 paper requires a much broader overview.

# REPRESENTATIONS

In this case the distinction between 'Media Representations' at AS and 'Representations' at A2 may seem a very subtle one, but important for all that. At AS you learnt what is meant by the media concept of 'representation' and to apply it to specific texts (MED1) and genres or media forms (MED2). Now, at A2, you are in a position to put that knowledge into practice, applying it to specific social groups and places and comparing one with another, perhaps across different media forms.

Application is the important idea here, the ability to take your knowledge and understanding and overlay it on both specific texts and a more general perception of society and culture and the ideologies therein. This is a sophisticated skill where, at best, you are able to range widely in overview and focus down hard on the detail of specific examples at will. We can describe this as being like working with both a telescope and a microscope.

Notice that the specification stipulates two studies of groups or places. This may form part of the wording of the exam questions and to access the full choice of questions it may be wise to prepare both groups and places. The fact that there are two studies gives the Principal Examiner the option to ask you to compare or contrast them so keep this in mind.

The specification repeatedly refers to 'images' in this section so you will need to focus on visual media, though it is not clear how literally the term should be taken. At the same time reference is made to 'a range of media' so make sure you have moving and still images to draw on at the least.

To answer the questions in this section successfully you need to engage early on with the notion of categorising the media's representations in various ways.

One popular approach that the specification alludes to is to link representation with ideology and categorise representations according to dominant and other ideologies in circulation.

What this means in practice is that the media represents the dominant sets of attitudes or belief systems that circulate in society. Occasionally minority views may be represented, though not necessarily supported in so doing. Sometimes we might be aware of other groups or places and prevalent attitudes towards them by their absence rather than their presence.

The term 'dominance' in terms of representations can be rather misleading. We all tend to believe that our view of the world is the 'normal' accepted one! The dominant view though is the one that would tend to find most support in mainstream society and be supported by hegemonic agencies such as the law, education, government and the media!

There may be significant sections of society that would not hold the 'dominant' view and you may well belong to one of them. Young people as a group tend not to be securely associated with the mainstream, though this notion in itself is perhaps a stereotypical representation!

Let's use a case study to examine this in a bit more detail:

## CASE STUDY

### MOTHERS

Strictly speaking mothers aren't really a social group, though they could be considered as an important subset of the social group of women!

Studies of gender representation are prone to some very hackneyed 'received wisdom' about gender politics and reading students' exam answers it's rare to hear their own voice in their responses. Nevertheless, gender representation is clearly such an important issue that it seems wrong to ignore it. See, for example, 'Slugs, Snails and Puppy Dogs Tails', a case study on representation and men in the A2 Essential Introduction.

Over the years many social groups have radically changed in the way they are represented in the media, and indeed, in society itself. Mothers, though, seem to endure in their archetypal role as nurturer and carer.

More and more taboos are broken and no longer thought shocking or sensational but the need for a mother to put her children first and care for them effectively remains enshrined at the heart of female gender representation.

Parenting is perhaps the one arena where it is socially accepted that women hold sway over men. Witness for example the support given to mothers by the courts in cases of separation and divorce where children are involved. Here we see the law supporting the hegemonic ideology that women are more effective carers of children than men.

Of course, far from good news, this is seen by some as another manifestation of patriarchy designed to oppress women by making them believe they are designed to nurture children rather than run the board room.

Nevertheless, motherhood is an area of our culture and society where positive female role models prevail and this makes it particularly interesting in terms of media representation.

It is no surprise that the great housewives' TV genre, soap opera, offers us many versions of motherhood. With their conservative ideologies of the importance of the family, soap operas place mothers, even matriarchs, at the centre of the community. In *EastEnders* Lou and then Pauline Fowler have occupied this role, endeavouring to keep the family together against all odds. Surrogate mother figures such as Mo Slater introduce a more maverick element into this equation. Characters such as Pat Butcher or Kat Slater represent motherhood-in-jeopardy with their, so-represented, rather warped sense of priorities. They are ultimately redeemed however by the power of other family members or the wider community to keep them on the ideological straight-and-narrow.

In this rather brief example you can perhaps see how different versions of motherhood are offered and function to stabilise certain ideological preferred readings.

The truly neglectful mother is a figure rarely seen in the media and when she does appear she generally must be excised as though a social cancer! Situation comedy is a genre that has offered more scope for alternative representations than soap opera and drama, perhaps because comedy can be used to reinforce dominant representations, alternatives functioning as the butt of the joke.

A good example of this phenomenon in action with regard to parenting can be found in the BBC show *The Royle Family*, written by and starring Caroline Aherne and Craig Cash. Set in Manchester, the show centres on a working class family, the Royles, the older generation of whom are represented very stereotypically along gender lines. Jim sits in his armchair-cum-throne with the remote control, cracking jokes and generally directing operations while Barbara, his wife, waits on him and sympathises with their children and her mother, the butts of Jim's jokes.

The younger generation represent a much more complex and confusing world of gender politics. Denise, the vain and lazy daughter, is married to Dave, a witless removal man. When they have baby David conventional gender roles are challenged to great comic effect.

Roles are reversed and Dave adopts the feminised role of nurturer, much to Jim's amusement. In one episode, 'The Christening', Dave comments that he can't go on a lads' do to Amsterdam because he's 'never left the baby on its own with Denise overnight before'. This neat re-working of the over-protective new mother amuses and endears us to Dave. However, it places Denise on dangerously dysfunctional ground. She tells the female company assembled in the kitchen at the party that she stopped breast feeding because it was 'more convenient for Dave to make up the bottles'! Denise is rescued from the outer-darkness of downright neglect though by her concern to improve as a mother. In a touching scene in the bedroom with baby David in the cot we see the otherwise feckless Dave counsel and encourage Denise in her mothering. 'What can I talk to him about?' she asks. 'Talk about your day', he replies . . . 'Oprah, Trisha, Ricki Lake?' she says quizzically. 'You see, you are a good mother after all', he soothes. We may laugh wryly at this but the juxtaposition of Denise with a guest character, Michelle, in this episode helps to maintain our sympathy for the floundering new mother.

Neale and Krutnik argued in their work on situation comedy that stereotyping sometimes takes such an extreme form that the character can be termed monstrous in their representation of attitudes and values which shock and alienate the audience and so enables them to laugh freely (Neale, S. and Krutnik, F. (1990), *Popular Film and Television Comedy*, London, Routledge).

Michelle is such a 'monstrous' character. She cheerfully admits to having her children taken into care and even to not knowing their ages 'and I don't bloody care love as long as they're not old enough to be prosecuted'. In her blokeishness

Michelle doesn't belong in the world of the female characters. This is demonstrated through the mise en scène: all the females wearing florals and pastels with the exception of Michelle who wears black and a biker's jacket.

The other women only laugh at Michelle's jokes out of politeness but voice their disapproval of her behind her back. The men seem to enjoy her company but ultimately show their disapproval of her, through private nicknames for example. She belongs nowhere and is approved of by no-one. Here we begin to see the special contempt which is reserved for the failed mother and consequently the high importance bestowed upon this social role, more perhaps in its absence than at any other time.

Denise's failings as a new mother pale into insignificance set against Michelle's negligence – a useful tool on the writers' part perhaps to retain sympathy for Denise, a regular and important character, not to mention at the same time perpetuating the myth of the self-abnegating mother.

A different but similar example could be found this summer in the local daily press in the North East of England, with stories of not one but two mothers abandoning their children making the headlines. Both stories were thought so sensational that they were picked up by the national and international press and in addition one of the mothers in question struck a deal with the gossip magazine *Closer*. A failing mother is big news apparently. But why?

The ancient archetype of the nurturing mother perhaps harks back to the need for a stable and secure environment in which children can be raised. Radical feminists might argue that such ideologies have been used to oppress women and stabilise the (patriarchal) economy by requiring women to care for children without payment. Certainly, some politicians have been complicit in creating very negative stereotypes around single mothers and even around career mothers who aim to combine challenging jobs with childcare responsibilities. So-called 'house husbands' who adopt roles traditionally belonging to women are viewed with scepticism in the media. Many adverts for cleaning products still ridicule the notion of men sharing domestic and childcare duties.

It is in this context that the news stories about mothers 'abandoning' children must be viewed. One of the women, Kelly Ann Piggford, left her three children under the age of five in the care of a 15-year-old babysitter while she went to Turkey for two weeks. The *Northern Echo*, the newspaper which broke the story, is unequivocal in its representation of the woman as a Proppian villain. The magistrate's judgment was blown up into large type, asserting 'you just put yourself first' – not in itself a crime but implicitly offered as a reminder of the selflessness a 'proper' mother should exhibit. Piggford's attempts to account for her actions in the magazine interview are represented by the newspaper as simply mercenary: 'for an undisclosed fee'. A later magazine interview, after her return, presents Piggford as more accepting of her hegemonic position: 'I will never leave my babies alone again' and is quoted in the newspaper at some length. It is interesting to reflect on the significance of the local newspaper and magazine's audience profiles and Piggford's opportunities for self-representation, given her power relative to the state and these media institutions.

In both publications it seems she is offered as an object of vilification or, at best, exotic strangeness with one headline running 'Fly-away mother'. In the second case of abandonment the child in question was 15 but the mother had absconded to be with her Turkish lover, 20 years her junior. Again, the 'strangeness' of the behaviour is highlighted: 'Lovestruck mother'.

These headlines seem to be offered to the readers as paradoxes or enigmas with the ideological function of implicitly re-affirming what a mother should be. Interestingly enough, several weeks later follow-up stories appeared which either re-confirmed the wrongness of the original behaviour by claiming the mother had re-offended or by asserting an alternative and preferable situation: 'Happy family at last for deserted daughter'. It is notable here that the notion of family is secured through the appearance of the fathers, previously absent, adopting some traditional female roles and, to an extent, being represented as victims of the mothers' outlandish behaviour: 'I am so sorry for what Mam has done to you'.

ACTIVITY

*Look at the three photographs and captions which were offered alongside the news stories. Analyse them in the light of the representational issues discussed above. How do they function to confirm the mothers as deviant and neglectful and how is this representation countered by the image of the 'new family'?*

# Happy family at last for deserted daughter

Together again: Laura with her father, George Wilthew, and his partner Diane McDowell

Picture: DAVID WOOD

**By OLIVIA RICHWALD**

A SCHOOLGIRL whose mother abandoned her to start a new life abroad last night said it was the best thing that has ever happened to her.

Fifteen-year-old Laura Wilthew was shocked when she returned home one day in July to find her mother, Elaine Walker, and sister Stacey, 17, had stripped the family house and moved to Turkey – without warning her.

The scandal made international headlines, and Miss Walker, from Redmire, near Leyburn, in North Yorkshire, was accused of being a monster by her teenage daughter.

But now, seven weeks after she was abandoned, Laura has been reunited with the father she had been banned from seeing for five years.

Laura and her father, George Wilthew, had last seen each other when she was ten, when Miss Walker walked out on Mr Wilthew, her husband for a decade.

But father and daughter were brought back together by social services after Miss Walker moved to Turkey.

Last night, speaking from their home in Louisa Street, Darlington, Laura said: "I just want to make a clean break and get on with my new life.

"When my mum left my dad, she told me I wasn't allowed to see him ever again, and I was so upset I used to cry every night.

"But this is the best thing that has ever happened to me in my life, because I am back with my dad."

Mr Wilthew and his partner, Diane McDowell, were on holiday in Turkey themselves when they heard about the abandonment.

Mr Wilthew said: "I was on the phone to my son, Peter, who was telling me about it when the news came on, and I saw her on the TV.

"It was a shock and I was surprised because people just don't leave their kids."

Laura said she was nervous when she learned she was to meet her father again.

She said: "Social services got me his number and I had really bad butterflies because I hadn't spoken to him for five years. But as soon as I saw him he was so nice and so was Diane. He was gobsmacked when he saw me."

Ms McDowell, who has been in a relationship with Mr Wilthew for three-and-a-half years, said: "He always talked about Laura and wanted to see her again, so he is very happy now."

On the night Miss Walker left Mr Wilthew, Laura wrote her father a note, which read: "I am so sorry for what mam has done to you. Someday we will get her back for what she has done to us. Love you to bits dad, and you will be alright with me, Grandad. Love you with all my heart, Laura."

Mr Wilthew kept the letter and picture in his wallet for five years – and when he showed it to his daughter when they were reunited, she burst into tears.

Earlier this month, on the first day of the new school term, Mr Wilthew drove Laura back to her old school, Wensleydale School, in Leyburn, but she broke down, unable to return to a place with such bad memories.

So this week she started at Eastbourne Comprehensive, in Darlington, just around the corner from her new home.

The family would like to see Miss Walker prosecuted.

Yesterday, a Crown Prosecution Service (CPS) spokeswoman said: "At this stage there will not be a prosecution, but it doesn't mean there never will be, they can always be reinvestigated.

"As far as CPS is concerned, we are not involved."

Laura has not heard from her mother or sister since they moved to Turkey to be with their holiday romance boyfriends.

Absent mother: Elaine Walker with her Turkish boyfriend

To Dad,
Thank you for everything and I am so sorry for what mam has done to you. But someday you will get her back for what she has done to us and you will be alright with me, and Grandad.
Love you with all my heart.
From Laura

Words of love: Laura's letter to her father

Figure 1: (left, and right) © The Northern Echo

A kiss for the cameras: Elaine Walker and her Turkish lover steal a kiss in front of the media yesterday

# Lovestruck mother: 'I'll never return'

By JOE WILLIS
and NICOLA JUNCAR

RUNAWAY mother Elaine Walker broke her silence last night and vowed never to come home to care for her teenage daughter.

Miss Walker, who denies abandoning 15-year-old Laura, said she will never return to Britain.

She said she was in love and plans to marry her boyfriend, Ali Murat, a DJ who is 20 years her junior.

Miss Walker, 45, from Redmire, near Leyburn, North Yorkshire, flew to Turkey

### Girl, 15, left at home as mum flies to her lover

Flashback: How The Northern Echo broke the story

with her other daughter, 17-year-old Stacey, nearly three weeks ago.

Both women are believed to have found boyfriends while on holiday in the country in June.

Speaking from the Turkish province of Gaziantep, Miss Walker said she had left her 15-year-old daughter with a relative.

She said: "My daughter didn't want to come because she had exams.

"She will come here for a holiday before the new year."

Miss Walker said she was prepared to risk everything to be with her lover.

"I fell madly in love with him at first sight.

"The age difference between us is completely unimportant. I won't return to Britain again."

Miss Walker and her boyfriend talked of plans to marry and how they had started to set up home together at his house in eastern Turkey.

With her boyfriend's arm draped around her, she said: "We first saw each other and liked each other. Then we would see each other every day.

"When I went home to England, I promised I would come back to Turkey to be with him.

"I did everything I could, and in three weeks I was coming back and now I'm staying with him, because I love him."

She also told how she made the first move.

"I came to Ali and told him I liked him. We sat and we talked and we knew we liked each other a lot."

Villagers in Redmire have spoken of their shock at her actions, but said her daughter is coping well.

It transpired that Miss Walker, who also has two grown-up children, had handed in her notice at work.

Laura is being cared for by relatives while waiting for her father, who is believed to live in Darlington, to return from abroad to be with her.

North Yorkshire Police said they would like to speak to Miss Walker. But a spokesman added yesterday it was still too early to say whether she would be prosecuted.

# Fly-away mother faces jail for neglect

By NICOLA JUNCAR

A YOUNG mother who left her three children in the care of a schoolgirl while she went on holiday has been warned she could face prison.

Kelly Ann Piggford, also known as Rogerson, pleaded guilty to three charges of child neglect at Darlington Magistrates' Court yesterday.

The 24-year-old, from Darlington, left her two sons and daughter with the teenager before jetting off to Turkey, a court heard.

While she partied with two friends in the popular resort of Marmaris, her children were staying with the girl in a one-bedroom flat.

Chairman of the bench Clement O'Donovan told Piggford: "The circumstances in which you left your children were wholly unacceptable by any standard.

"As a parent, you have failed in your responsibility to look after your children.

"By your guilty plea you accept your arrangements for your children were inadequate – you just put yourself first. Your children were placed at risk."

He added: "We are not sentencing you today, but instead have asked for a pre-sentence report. The steering we give is for a custodial sentence, because we view these charges as being so serious."

Depending on the outcome of the report, Piggford could still be sentenced at crown court.

The court heard how Piggford had just returned from a holiday in Turkey, on June 6, before jetting off again.

The first time she went on

holiday, she took her daughter and left her sons with their father.

But only four days after her return, she booked a second two-week holiday at the same resort with two friends.

Christopher Williamson, prosecuting, said Piggford claimed a former partner had assaulted her, and this was why she was returning to Turkey.

On June 13, she went on her second holiday and the children were left in the one-bedroom flat.

After staying there for three nights, the landlady found out and asked them to leave, saying the situation was inappropriate.

The children were then taken to the house of one of the friends whom Piggford was on holiday with.

Mr Williamson said: "Social services became aware of the problem and attended that property.

"There they found another woman looking after (the friend's) two-year-old daughter, as well as the babysitter and the children of Kelly Rogerson."

The case made national headlines after The Northern Echo reported how police and social services had intervened following complaints by a neighbour.

While on holiday, Piggford gave an interview to a magazine for an undisclosed fee. She said: "You see 15-year-old mothers, so why not have 15-year-old babysitters? I don't understand the fuss."

> "
As a parent, you have failed in your responsibility to look after your children. By your guilty plea you accept your arrangements for your children were inadequate – you just put yourself first. Your children were placed at risk
>
> ### Chairman of the bench Clement O'Donovan

Despite claims she was trying to catch a flight home, Piggford did not return for another 11 days, when she was arrested by police who met her at Durham Tees Valley Airport.

On her arrival, she gave another magazine interview in which she said: "I will never leave my babies alone again.

"Seeing them has made me feel so guilty, but I promise I will make it up to them and I will always be there in future."

In mitigation, Chris Bunting asked for Piggford's early guilty plea to be taken into account and said her children were well and back in her care.

He said: "This was not a case of abandonment. Clothes and nappies had been left with

Threat of prison: Kelly Ann Piggford arrives at court – to hear she might be going to jail

the babysitter and money was available to buy food.

"The children appeared quite content."

He said social services officers had made visits to Piggford on several occasions since the children were returned to her, and seemed

happy with the situation.

Their visits had been regular, but were now happening only once a fortnight.

Piggford will be back at Darlington Magistrates' Court on September 1. Her unconditional bail was extended.

A Darlington resident who

lives on the same estate as Piggford, and who did not wish to be named, said: "She doesn't deserve to have the children. There are some families who try for years to have children but can't, and then you get people like her."

➤ Comment – Page 12

Most of the specification demands for this topic area have been addressed through this case study.

The first three bullet points:

- A detailed study of a group across a range of media
- Alternative images of these groups
- General issues of representation and stereotyping

are clearly text-based and really allow you to work in a way fairly similar to that at AS.

The second three:

- Problems of producing fair and accurate representations
- Representation and power
- Reasons for dominant representations

are much more challenging and really underline the fact that AO2 is the dominant Assessment Objective (AO) for this paper (with AO3 also playing a prominent role).

So, at AS

**Key Concepts** ⟵ **Texts** ⟶ **Ideas/Theories**

But at A2

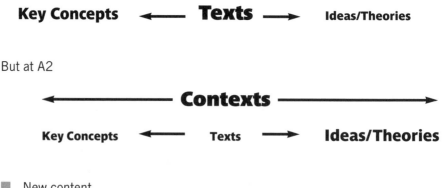

- New content
- New concepts
- AND a re-weighting of concepts familiar at AS

NOT how texts work (as at AS)

BUT why texts are the way they are.

Texts remain important, of course, but the way they are used is likely to change. Central at AS, texts at A2 act as the means through which ideas can be explored, or as evidence to support a hypothesis or argument.

Note how in the mothers' case study, pages 55–9, the argument comes first – the dominant media representation of mothers is as nurturing and self-abnegating – and this is supported and extended through textual examples, among which, ideally, you will range freely. A really accomplished answer will have this ability to take examples from a range of media sources and use them either in detail or in passing, as required.

Part of the skill here is being able to identify a range of appropriate examples that will be useful to you. Broad, varied and extensive media consumption becomes of critical importance as a differentiator here. This will almost certainly involve you in watching, reading and listening to texts you wouldn't by choice.

Equally, you must take an active approach to your own media consumption and 'box clever' to apply it to your examination answers. Start from what you are familiar with if possible as this will save you time.

For example, in terms of this topic area and representations of place the USA seems a good bet – so many texts originate from there and depict representations of it that you should be spoilt for choice! You could map your own recent media consumption that provides you with representations of the USA. (See page 64.)

Such is the vast media output from USA that you could probably restrict yourself to one form (e.g. film), or genre (e.g. television sitcom) and still have a good range of representations. Furthermore, its status as an elite nation means that it features heavily every day in UK news. All of this makes it a particularly interesting choice of focus in respect of the topic area's final three specific demands:

- Fairness and accuracy
- Power
- Explaining dominant representations.

There are a variety of possible 'ways-in' to tackling these issues and ultimately they should probably be dealt with together.

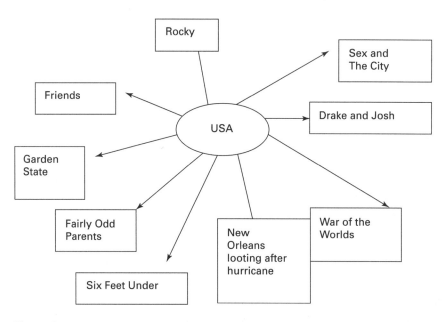

**Figure 2**

One approach could be through the key concepts:

## INSTITUTION

The power of commercial vested interest militates against fairness and accuracy unless this makes commercial sense. The prominence of the USA as a media producer means that the interests of wealthy white males exert an undue influence in the representations produced. US media imperialism can be seen to promote myths about America across the world, encouraging other nations to adopt its ideologies, to appropriate its values and lifestyles; in short to 'consume' it whilst at the same time bestowing more power and status upon it.

## AUDIENCE

While notions of fairness and accuracy in representations may be deemed important in an abstract sense it is quite possible to argue that they are not found to be so in practice, certainly not in comparison to notions of escapism or entertainment. For example, some audiences may prefer to have their stereotypical perceptions reinforced and confirmed rather than challenged or threatened. Likewise institutions may promote this attitude because trading in stereotypes can save them time and money.

## GENRE

An easy-going sitcom like *Friends* represents the USA as an affluent land of opportunity, urban and stylish, populated by white, heterosexual, attractive, well-adjusted aspirers. Deviations from the norm the show sets up, such as Susan, Ross's former wife, who is a lesbian, are treated with scepticism and at some distance from the central group of characters with whom we are encouraged to empathise and laugh.

The more demanding comic drama *Six Feet Under* offers its audience a fundamentally more idiosyncratic and dysfunctional representation of modern-day USA, where myths of the American dream are questioned and satirised. Interestingly enough however, the programme retains the rather archaic notion of 'the family business' and 'family home' amidst an apparent complete breakdown of sexual and social norms. It remains unclear to the viewer, perhaps, whether this is a reflexive ironic comment on the genre or a serious and necessary 'nod' to the Establishment and mainstream propriety. After all, the show is made by HBO, a subsidiary of Time Warner, the largest media corporation of all time!

## VALUES AND IDEOLOGY

In modern US media texts social fragmentation and threats to the archetypal nuclear family are almost universally acknowledged. However, this acknowledgement is often more tacit or cosmetic than real and deep-rooted. In the recent re-make of *War of The Worlds* Tom Cruise – a clean-cut, blue-eyed boy if ever there was one – is portrayed at the outset as a single parent, a weekend dad, and a charmless and inept one at that! Presumably this updating of the original is intended to convince the audience of the realism and accuracy of the film's representations.

This inauspicious start doesn't prevent him, however, from ultimately assuming a hero-like status in saving his daughter from invading aliens and providing his son with the wherewithal to fight alongside the US army, to oust the aliens and safely return to his mother's home where the 'family' are, at least nominally, 're-united'. Herein we see that the ideology of family is alive and well in the US media, even if the actual composition of family groupings is metamorphosing.

In the children's cartoon *Fairly Odd Parents*, Timmy, an only child, is seen to experience a sort of low level neglect by his parents and is often cared for by a cruel babysitter, Vicky. He is protected and fulfilled by his relationship with his fairy godparents who compensate for the inadequacies of other aspects of Timmy's life. The ideological significance of all this is unlikely to be lost on the modern child: 'I wish my parents spent more time with me!' The drive behind the narrative of almost every episode is that the parents learn the error of their ways and offer Timmy a more fulfilling family life.

So, in summary, at the same time that US media texts are offering us modern and 'accurate' representations they are pedalling ideological anachronisms.

But why does the notion of a wholesome family set-up continue to exert such a hold on institutions and, by implication, audiences in the face of the reality of social fragmentation? Possible reasons might include:

- A historic norm
- A political convenience
- Economically beneficial
- Social cementation

Think back to the three bullet points under consideration:

- Fairness and accuracy
- Power
- Reasons for dominant representations

Hopefully you can see how the textual examples above address these issues.

To end this section let's think a little more closely about the examination's demands. For each topic you have a choice of two questions and must answer one of them.

Look at past papers on www.aqa.org.uk and consider the differences between the two questions:

- Equal difficulty
- Test different aspects of the specification
- Varying focus: broad or more directed

■ May be 'hung' on a quote

■ Require textual examples, even if this isn't explicit

You need to attempt answers to different sorts of questions to see which suits you better. As a fail-safe work towards coping with your less-preferred style of question! Check you understand the terminology of the questions so that you don't feel uncertain about the appropriateness of your response.

You don't really want to be in a situation where you are forced to answer one question because you are unprepared for the topic material on the other.

■ A range of theories and issues should be understood.

■ Some detailed knowledge will be needed.

■ Be prepared to apply that knowledge so that you use what you know to engage the examiner, construct an argument and generate some sort of debate.

Here's an example using a brainstorm and plan answer to a question from June 2005:

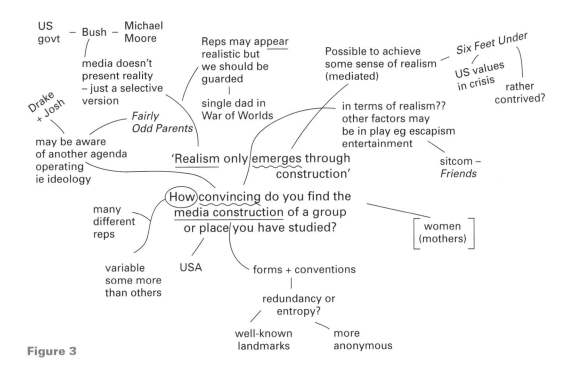

**Figure 3**

**2b** '**Realism only emerges through construction.**'

**How convincing do you find the media construction of a social group or place that you have studied?**

**AQA June 2005**

Break the question down and reflect on any issues arising:

■ Question more important than quotation.

■ Quotation seems to be used to 'round out' the question . . . it might give some leads.

■ Requires one example: group or place, so headline this in introductory paragraph.

Order the points from the spidergram making sure there are different and appropriate textual examples for each paragraph/point.

1 Many different representations contribute to the notion of the media's construction of USA. Some are much more convincing than others in relation to realism, but there are other purposes at work in texts so may 'convince' in other ways.

2 No media text presents reality, only re-presents a selective version of it. Compare Bush on news vs. Moore's depiction of him in *Farenheit 9/11*.

3 Some texts may seem to work hard to convince us of their realism but we should be on our guard, e.g. *War of The Worlds* re-make.

4 We may be aware that there is an agenda on the part of the producer and or audience that is driving the representation, e.g. the perceived importance of promoting family values to children, even where this doesn't always reflect their reality: *Fairly Odd Parents*, *Drake and Josh*.

5 But it is possible to achieve some sense of realism, albeit mediated, e.g. *Six Feet Under*.

6 The quote implies realism is of paramount importance in representations but not true: stereotypes provide easy identification and so save time and money. Audiences want to escape, to be entertained and perhaps have their views confirmed e.g. *Friends*, *Rocky*.

7 Conclusion. How convincing? Variable. Our view is developed through a process of accretion of many texts which might enhance our scepticism or faith in the representations we see.

NOTE

## ALTERNATIVES INC.

When we find alternative representations of groups or places in the media it can be pleasing and refreshing, especially if they seem to oppose the prevailing dominant ideology and challenge hegemony in some way. In some cases though these alternatives have been appropriated by those in power in order to control the threat they pose. This process is termed *Incorporation*.

Sports clothing manufacturers who know the cultural value of cool black opinion leaders have incorporated black male ideologies of individualism and non-conformism into their marketing strategies. By re-packaging and absorbing ideas that run counter to their own commercial and oligarchic vested interests their impact is reduced or their power annexed for other (corporate) ends.

A rather more anarchic version of incorporation can be seen in the attempts by oppressed minorities to appropriate and re-direct the language of their oppression, originally controlled and operated by other (dominant) groups. In so doing the minority group seeks to dilute or deflect the power of this language to oppress, to change the stereotypical representation. This trend can be observed among male and female homosexuals and among some black Americans who have appropriated terms such as 'pimp' and 'nigger', much to the horror of their politically correct white counterparts.

Let's finish by considering how you might approach the pair of questions that were set in January 2004. They were:

a    Does media stereotyping always marginalise whole groups of people? Illustrate your answer with examples.

b    'Media representations of the world can appear so natural that we can easily see them as real.' Discuss this quote with reference to one social group or place that you have studied.

January 2004 AQA

You should see immediately that these are two very different questions and that the possibility of a one-size-fits-all response is simply not on the cards for either.

Both are asking for a specific understanding of the nature of representation and both require appropriate exemplification if your arguments are going to stand up. Which you tackle will obviously be determined by which you feel most confident you can answer well.

Both are demanding questions in their different ways, so there is no question of one being easier than the other. One differentiator that you might note is that while the first question allows for either a broad overview with possibly a wide range of examples or alternatively an approach that might be focused on a more narrow range of examples, the second question directly demands that you address the issue from the perspective of just one social group or place. The implication for the second question is that you need in-depth knowledge of one specific example of representation. Let's have a look at where you might take these questions in your responses.

A logical place to begin with question (a) is a definition. What exactly do we mean by 'stereotyping'? You might like to think around ideas of 'shortcuts used by the media to characterise groups'. You might like to consider including in your definition the way in which groups of people are represented by a few or even just one characteristic, which becomes a means of pigeonholing them and even predicting their behaviour. Stereotyping is often seen as both negative and offensive because it seeks to deny the complexity of people as human beings and reduces them to two-dimensional caricatures.

Next you might consider what type of group it is that we see most often stereotyped in the media. This is quite a complex question because not all groups who are stereotyped are necessarily represented negatively. Try to think of some examples of positive and negative representations in this way. Also representations and stereotypes are far from static and change over a period of time. However, in traditional media terms one can say that in general stereotypes tend to be of minority groups, such as ethnic groups, gays, and people from predominantly working class areas such as the East End of London, or at least the East End as it was before house prices rocketed.

Many of these groups, especially ethnic minorities, are stereotyped because society generally and the media specifically does not take the trouble to understand their cultural differences. Sections of the media, such as the popular press, use stereotypes as a shorthand way of describing people who belong to these groups. At times, however, there is clearly a wilful demonising of both individuals and groups to represent them as a threat to the stability of society. Certainly this type of stereotyping where blame is laid on specific groups has the effect of marginalising them by undermining their credibility and standing within our culture. You should be able to find lots of examples of groups that have been demonised and subsequently marginalised. Of course, part of this process one might argue is ideological. It gives the ruling elite someone to blame for the ills of society. The most extreme example of this was the rise of anti-Semitism in Nazi Germany. In doing so it diverts people from real issues and offers them scapegoats. Try looking at the reporting in the popular press of issues like social benefits for asylum seekers.

You might want to follow up this sort of point by exploring the inaccuracy of many stereotypes and how hard it is to correct these inaccuracies. Gay men for example are not all effeminate in the same way that all effeminate men are not gay despite what homophobic elements of the media would suggest.

Consider what stereotyping tells is about power relations within our society. One of the most heavily stereotyped groups in the past has been women. You have some good examples above to explore some of the ways that women are marginalised and therefore denied a power base within our society.

Finally you might consider some of the ways in which the media has sought to bring a more positive approach to the representation of minority groups. Media organisations such as the BBC have a policy of actively recruiting staff from under-represented groups in order to even out the imbalance of, for example, members of ethnic minorities on our television screens. You might, however, argue that this is mere tokenism, an example of top show that does nothing to change the fundamental imbalance of power for these groups.

These ideas should provide you with a framework for tackling this type of question. Try planning out with some appropriate examples that you have found in your studies.

As we have pointed out, question (b) makes rather more specific demands. If you are going to have a go at it, you need to be armed with some good detailed information about a social group or place. Of course there is no need to remind you that this is not an open invitation to write down everything you know about the representation of one of these. The focus of the question is very clear – we are looking at the process of mediation and how it creates the illusion of realism.

Note that this question is very close to the example we have worked above based on the June 2005 paper.

The trick to writing a good response to this type of essay lies in linking the theoretical perspectives on the question, issues of realism and manipulation with good use of examples. The example given above of the USA would fit very well as an approach to this question. It is the premise here that is rather different, so you need to be able to modify your material to fit in with that. In essence what you are looking at in these questions could be planned out as follows.

Media language, especially moving images, tends to be concerned with creating visual messages. These messages rely heavily on iconic signs. These work through their similarity with the things they represent. Hence much media output looks real because it imitates things that are real.

The media also plays a game of pretending to be real. Television programmes no matter how much they are rehearsed are made to look spontaneous. The whole idea of continuity editing is to get rid of the seams in visual narrative so that audiences do not see how it has been stitched together.

If you want to broaden the focus from moving images, you can look at the way in which all media texts are a process of selection, prioritising and editing. You might explore how the system of values implicit in the process creates the ideological work of a text. Newspapers and other print media might be a good example if they fit in with the group/place you are intending to exemplify.

Although the question does not ask for it, you could well end with a paragraph of the inherent dangers of this naturalising process in terms of hidden values and ideological function.

# GENRE

Like representation and audience, genre is an odd choice of topic for the MED4 as like the other two it is also a Key Concept that underpins all of the work that you do for the AQA A level qualification. However, like both representation and audience it allows you plenty of scope for exploring some of the wider issues and theoretical perspectives that are so important to your success in this unit.

Genre as a topic, however, is not without its dangers. The chief danger that any exploration of genre poses is that you do not get anywhere. There is a potential circularity in genre study which says in essence: these texts share certain features in common. Because these texts share these features in common they belong to the same genre. Texts which have the same features in common belong to the same genre.

**NOTE**

Don't forget that the concept of genre has an application well beyond the confines of the moving image. This is one opportunity on the specification for you to explore other areas of media output, for example popular music.

You will see immediately that this approach severely limits the usefulness of genre as a critical tool. It is a good idea, therefore, to try to establish some sense of why genre is such an important concept when applied to a study of the media. To do this it is probably best to look at three key functions of genre.

First genre is an important concept to the producers of media texts, although you will probably hear very few of them ever speak of it. Media texts, as you should know by now, are largely the products of industrial processes. They are created for mass consumption and in most cases have been created in order to make a profit. Most media products require the investment of money, equipment, technology and human resources if they are to see the light of day. Most are particularly dependent on expensive plant and equipment such as studios and printing presses. Failure in the sense of creating products that do not appeal to mass audiences is expensive. Success on the other hand can bring rich rewards. Genre is one way of helping to know and predict what audiences will find appealing. Genre is another way of describing winning formulas that stand at least some chance of appealing to audiences.

NOTE

In television production, the word 'format' is often used to describe a particular type of programme which in Media Studies we might describe as a genre or sub-genre. Quiz shows therefore are a particular format which distinguish them from other types of television programme such as situation comedies.

Of course for producers it is not simply a matter of continually repeating a winning formula in order to achieve success. Audiences soon tire of predictable formulas and will be quick to abandon tired clichéd formats. Part of the producers' game has to be to know how to refresh a particular genre formula so that it remains recognisable but has sufficient innovation to make it new and interesting to the jaded palates of the audiences.

ACTIVITY

*Choose a genre with which you are familiar and trace its development over a period of time. This is likely to be quite a short period of time with some genres and rather longer with others. Try to identify some of the important milestones when key developments have taken place. For example if you are looking at situation comedy, you might look at such series as Hancock's Half Hour, Steptoe and Son, Fawlty Towers, The Young Ones and Blackadder as some of the key defining moments in the development of this television genre.*

*Now take a look at some of the contemporary examples of output in this genre and try to identify:*

- *How it has developed*

- *What it might owe to those series outlined above*

- *What cultural and social forces might have influenced changes that have taken place in the genre*

Genre is also an important concept when it is used to examine the way in which audiences behave. Genre provides audiences with an immediate opportunity to recognise what they are buying into when they are considering whether to consume a media product. Indeed many outlets for media products are organised so that audiences can easily locate the genre that they are looking for. Newsagents organise their print products into specific sub-genres, such as women's magazines, sports magazines and the music press. Your local video shop similarly categorises films into genres: horror, thrillers and rom-coms. Record stores often arrange CDs into musical genres as well as alphabetically according to the name of the artists. Genre is a short cut to potential pleasure for audiences in many ways. First, it offers some guarantee that the product will contain ingredients with which the consumer is familiar and knows s/he enjoys. Second, the audience for a genre already knows many of the basic conventions of the genre so that this familiarity offers not only the pleasure of recognition but also a short cut to understanding and appreciating the text itself. The more familiar an audience is with the codes and conventions employed by a genre, the easier it is for them to read the text and potentially see more subtle nuances that might be lost on a reader unfamiliar with the genre. Indeed it can be argued that familiarity with a genre invites people to play games with the texts.

Finally in terms of the value of genre in Media Studies, we have its potential as a critical tool for analysing media texts. Media texts generally belong to a category of cultural artefacts that we would label popular culture. Besides signalling their popular appeal, this also indicates that these texts are generally not considered to be of lasting value but are created for immediate mass consumption. They are in fact the opposite of texts such as classic novels, operas and plays which we would categorise as high culture. These text tend to be of lasting value and are also worthy of detailed study in their own right. So for example Shakespeare's *Hamlet* might be set for study as a single text at A level. An episode of *Coronation Street* probably would not.

What genre does then is to allow us to lump together 'popular' texts and study them collectively as a group. For study in MED4 this provides you with an excellent opportunity to move on from the analysis of individual texts and enables you to consider the broader implications of a group of texts belonging to the same genre. For example you may look at sitcoms as a genre rather than as individual texts and take the opportunity to tease out what these texts tell us about the social, political and economic conditions when they were first broadcast. For example, how far does *The Young Ones* reflect on the Thatcher years of the 1980s with its attendant Yuppiedom and obsession with individuality at the expense of society?

The current obsession with reality TV both on television itself and in print media such as magazines and popular newspapers might similarly provide an opportunity for study into some of the social, cultural and economic forces that have led to such an abundance of such programmes. Certainly the need to fill air time with popular but inexpensive programmes in light of the proliferation of channels following digitalisation would be an interesting avenue to explore. Similarly we might consider the voyeuristic nature of our culture given the explosion of media saturation through both digital channels and the Internet, a medium that allows us all the potential of media exposure in every sense of the word. So you can see that although individual texts such as Big Brother might not be of great importance individually, collectively they can tell us a great deal about the society and culture in which we live. They do this by acting as a kind of barometer to measure the state of our culture and our society, helping us determine the things that we value most and, perhaps more importantly, the things we value the least.

It is important that you try to bear these three aspects of genre in mind when you come to tackle an exam question on this topic. Even if all three are not directly relevant to the question, you should at least be aware of them so as to avoid closing down and limiting your response to one that simply asserts the nature of genre rather than identifying some of its functions.

The specification offers just four bullet points under the subject content for genre. You do of course have its definition in terms of a Key Concept to take into account as well when preparing your exam response.

The first bullet point requires you to consider the codes and conventions of one genre from any medium/media. That means you have a pretty vast field to choose from, potentially the entire media output of the world. You may well to limit this to looking at a genre that you already know, perhaps one that you have studied at AS level, say in film and broadcast fiction. Equally you may see this as an opportunity to develop your interest in the media into an area that particularly captures your imagination or holds your interest. Of course, there is an interesting tension here between what you might want to do and what our teacher thinks is appropriate. You should, however, have given some thought to your own interests in preparing your MED5 independent study. Your teacher will feel much more confident in your ability to explore and develop ideas for yourself if you have proved your ability to do so by working independently and effectively on your coursework. If you are really smart you will choose a MED5 topic that will enable you to prepare some of the work that you need for this topic at the same time. It is certainly an opportunity to seek out and use a short cut.

In order to get at the codes and conventions of one genre, you need to be reasonably selective in deciding which texts you are going to look at. An encyclopaedic sweep of the whole output of one particular genre will take you too far away from the individual texts to be of any real value. Better to take a detailed look at a smaller number of specific texts. One reason for this is that you may well need in the exam question to present textual evidence to support the points your are making. Some abstract survey of genre is not something that will help you. It is probably a good idea to start with a grid like the one in the activity box on the next page which is designed for use with moving image texts such as film and television programmes. In it you should identify some of the most significant codes and conventions to be found within the genre you are studying and for each one note down a couple of examples from texts you have studied. You may even wish to further elaborate on this task by looking for evidence of the way in which these conventions may have changed over a period of time, by choosing examples from different eras of the genre.

An important convention that hopefully you are conversant with is iconography. This is an extension of the mise en scène. Iconography refers to those recurring elements of the mise en scène that define the genre. They may include settings, props and costumes. So for the British gangster movie, the East End pub, sharp suits, guns and flash cars are all elements of the iconography that identify and define this particular sub-genre. They provide immediately recognisable clues for the audience and a valuable short cut for the producer.

Narrative should allow you to explore similarly the conventions of your chosen genre. Narrative outcome is often helpful here as the way in which a narrative ends is frequently specific to the genre: musicals with a grand finale, gangster films with a shoot-out, the rom-com with a wedding or at least the promise of one. Other more subtle devices are worth looking at, for example in soaps the use of multi-strand narratives and parallel action to provide the audience with a privileged position in relation to the characters.

Consider these conventions and complete the grid by adding some examples.

| Convention | Example |
| --- | --- |
| Narrative structure/features | |
| Character typology | |
| Themes | |
| Settings/mise en scène | |
| Iconography | |
| Representation | |
| Ideology and values | |
| Audience appeal | |

The characters themselves are often familiar between texts within a genre offering variations on a specific theme. Rather than simply listing the similarities, it is useful to explore why such similar characters appear across texts within a genre. Soap operas for example often represent female characters as being both strong and yet vulnerable presumably in order to maintain their appeal to the largely female audience. How far do you feel that this is an accurate representation of life in twenty-first-century Britain or do you feel that the writers of soaps are using licence in creating characters to appeal to their audience? Soaps have traditionally focused on the idea of geographical community, the East End of London, Liverpool or Manchester perhaps as a substitute for the real communities that many see as fast disappearing. However, with the creation of communities in reality TV shows, it is interesting to see if fictional characters will be able to continue to compete with 'real' people for the voyeuristic attentions of their audiences.

Certainly the second bullet point in the specification, historical development of the genre, might offer you some interesting opportunities to explore the way in which texts within a genre have changed in light of the context in which they are produced and consumed. If you are studying a genre like soap, it is important that you get access to an early episode and make a careful study of it in relation to a recently broadcast episode. Again the grid on page 78 would be a useful way of identifying some of the basic changes that have taken place within the genre. For example if you look at narrative and themes, present-day soaps are likely to have far more dramatic and, some would say, far-fetched, storylines than their earlier counterparts. Similarly some of the themes that modern soaps tackle through their storylines would be considered much more sensational and risqué to an audience 30 years ago. Try to collect some examples of these changes that have taken place over the years for your chosen genre and try to relate them closely to textual evidence from texts that you have actually seen. Don't rely on textbooks to tell you – there is every chance that the textbook will be out of date anyway.

There is a real pitfall to avoid in this bullet point – that is, the approach where you decide that regardless of the question you are going to write everything there is to say about the development of a genre. What you end up with is a contrived and usually inappropriate historical survey of a genre with little reference to texts to support your viewpoint. The Western is a particular danger area for two reasons.

1   As a genre, the Western attracted the attention of many genre theorists in the 1960s and 1970s. In consequence there is a vast amount of literature about the Western genre written at that time. Although this work contributed greatly to genre theory and provides valuable background reading it is very much limited in its application to other film and moving image genres.

2   Very few significant Westerns have been made for over ten years now, so the availability of contemporary texts is rather limited. In fact, some would argue that Clint Eastwood's *Unforgiven* (1992) drew a line under the genre.

So you can see that to revise effectively for this topic, it is important that you adopt a workable approach to exploring the development of your chosen genre. This means first of all choosing a genre that will give you appropriate scope.

Have a look at the case study of the crime fiction on page 251 *Genre in A2 Media Studies: The Essential Introduction*. This should give you some idea of how you can explore the development in light of some of the wider contexts that may have influenced the kind of texts which have been produced as part of it. Don't, however, us this as a crib sheet for the exam. Use it as a guide to how you might look at a genre of your own choosing, or if you are going to use crime fiction. As your genre, make sure you use different examples from the ones in that chapter. Examiners are not impressed by candidates who simply copy out textbooks.

Don't forget that the texts that you will have engaged with as part of your work on MED5 will all belong to one genre or another so there may be a logic to using these as a basis for some exploration of this topic.

The third item in the subject content requires you to look at the wider contexts mentioned above and to identify reasons for the rise and fall in popularity of a genre. This is simply not something you can busk on the day of the exam. It needs careful thought and preparation if you are to attempt it at all. Having said that, it is potentially a fascinating area of research and one that, as we have suggested, can well be linked to your MED5 essay.

It is always a good idea with any work that you do for this specification to make the texts you have chosen the starting point and preparing for this topic on MED4 is no exception. The worst types of essays candidates produce for this topic ignore the texts completely and provide a learned and contrived overview of the wider contexts that have influenced the development of a genre. Many as a result also fail to examine contemporary texts. It is a good idea to make contemporary texts your starting point. This will allow you to get a grip on the contemporary influences that are at play in shaping contemporary texts within the genre. This will then provide you with an insight into the relationship between texts and contexts that is likely to be invaluable when you explore more historical examples which are more remote from your own personal experience.

For instance, if you are looking at sitcoms as an example of a television genre then begin by looking closely at half a dozen contemporary sitcoms. Try to make sure you explore a range as well. Start with a popular prime time example from ITV1 or BBC1 and then work your way into some of the more esoteric cult sitcoms broadcast on minority channels. At the same time try to determine what it is about the themes of these programmes that reflect the nature of present-day society.

The last bullet point in the subject content links closely with the work that you have just done on genre development. You are asked to consider recent developments in genre which include parody, pastiches, playing with genre conventions and mixing genres, or hybridity. If you are clued up on your theory, you will immediately identify a number of postmodern perspectives to be explored here. You might also realise that this is a rich seam in which to explore the topic of genre, not least because it can be seen as central to the issue of how valuable genre theory is to

Media Studies at a time when traditional notions of genre have become fragmented and genres so readily transmute and combine in face of the demand for more and more media output to fill time and space.

First you need to understand both the meaning of parody and pastiche. They are terms that are central to the ideas of Fredric Jameson, the American postmodern theorist. Jameson makes an important distinction between the two terms. Parody is a deliberate attempt to make fun of another text by imitating it and usually by exaggerating elements of it. Horror films provide a rich vein in which you can explore the use of parody. You should immediately be able to think up several contemporary examples in the horror and other film genres in which texts parody other texts. Use the grid below to tease out some of the ways in which this is done.

| Text 1 | Text 2 |
|---|---|
| Conventions | |
| Narrative | |
| Character | |
| Themes | |
| Iconography | |

ACTIVITY

Parody is close to satire. Satire seeks to point out absurdity and folly and to deflate pomposity. Parody seeks to point out and mock those things which it considers worthy of contempt.

Pastiche on the other hand has no such noble intent. For Jameson, pastiche is the simple copying, or ripping off, from texts that have been created previously. Pastiche just recycles texts from the past and in some cases passes these off as new. Of course, this is a difficult area not least because it raises also the issue of 'homage' where a film director copies the style of an existing film as a show of reverence for the achievement of a successful director of the past. Pop videos are an interesting place to explore the ideas of pastiche.

It is very much in the nature of postmodernism as a critical perspective that it identifies this role of recycling texts from the past not least to satisfy the ever-increasing media spaces that demand to be filled. So pastiche is in a sense a more cynical approach than parody which can be seen as a rather more worthy means of imitating previously produced texts. It is a worthwhile activity to collect examples of both of these types of texts from the genre that you are looking at to use as the basis for an essay which might ask you to consider how the two are different.

Other issues relating to the development of genre include hybridity or 'mixing genres' as the specification calls it. It is important to realise that one of the problems with genre study is that genres are generally not watertight categories. If they were then a lot of very boring genre texts would have been produced and audiences would have quickly tired of these. Genres keep themselves alive by evolving as you will have seen when you looked at the development of a genre. One way in which they evolve is by drawing upon other genres to feed into them. The obvious example is the docu-soap whose very name suggests the fusion of two established genres, the documentary and the soap opera.

The docu-soap also provides an interesting opportunity to explore wider contexts. The docu-soap came about as an answer to the need to develop cheap television programming in response to deregulation and the need to fill hours of airtime brought about by the arrival of digital technology. Soaps and documentaries are both expensive to produce. The former need stars and production facilities; the latter need an investment of time and resources for research and filming. Creating a genre that employs a cheap resource such as members of the public and films them in 'real life' situations, drives down costs and enables air time to be filled relatively cheaply. Add then a dimension of interactivity enabled by the development of digital technology and you can start indirectly charging audiences to view the programme further reducing costs by adding revenue. Thus the genre of reality television is born out financial and technological imperatives. Link to this a society which has become obsessed with surveillance and celebrity and it is easy to see that there is almost an inevitability about the advent of reality television.

---

*Choose another example of a recently developed genre and explain what you feel are some of the forces that have impacted on its development.*

ACTIVITY

---

The idea of playing with genre is also signalled in the specification. This again is a postmodern concept. It implies a deliberate attempt on the part of a film-maker for example to play with the notion of genre often by playing with the audience's expectations of a genre. A director like Quentin Tarantino, for example, in *Kill Bill* plays with the conventions of the martial arts genre with its traditions of revenge and fast fight sequences, not least by making the hero of the film a woman.

Tarantino provides an interesting example of an 'auteur'. In many ways auteur theory stands in opposition to genre theory suggesting as it does that many texts, particularly films, are identifiable more by the personal signature of their director than their adherence to a particular genre. Certainly the way in which Tarantino movies play with genre expectations and subvert them is typical of the personal signature that he adds to his films.

You might find it helpful in preparing for the exam to consider other ways in which producers and directors play with genre conventions and select examples of this from texts in your chosen genre.

Let's have a look at the types of questions that have previously been asked on the MED4 paper under the topic of genre.

In June 2004 the questions were:

a **'Genre arouses the expectations of an audience.' How and why does it do this?**

b **'Genres must adapt in order to survive.' Discuss.**

**AQA June 2004**

Two deceptively simple questions, both of which might be answered on a number of levels from the most simple to the extremely complex. This is typical of the problems posed by this topic in MED4 exams. Obviously, your first job when confronted by two such questions is to decide which one is the more appropriate for you to tackle. Unlike questions in other topics, there is no really obvious differentiation between the two in terms of the demands that they might make on your knowledge of genre. The first requires you to explore how genre arouses audience expectations while the second asks you to explore how genres adapt over a period of time. You might well use the same texts that you have studied for this topic to answer either of the questions. The key factor in determining which one you attempt is going to be your knowledge of either genre's relationship with audience or genre development.

> **NOTE**
>
> It is a quality of questions in this section, and of the paper generally, that they can look deceptively simple. Part of the problem that confronts the Principal Examiner who sets the exam is that genre is potentially such a wide area for candidates to study that questions have to be able to allow a wide variety of different responses. If they did not, then the paper might be very unfair to a significant number of people taking the exam. In consequence questions, particularly in this section, tend to appear very simple so they can give access to a wide range of answers. This is in part because they have to be quite general rather than asking for specifics. It is up to you as a candidate to supply the specifics. So your first job is to decipher the question and decide what aspect of genre you are being asked to explore. Then you need to consider just how you can use the material you have prepared in answering the question. For example if the question asks you to look at the rise and fall in popularity of a genre and you have prepared material on the gangster movie, then you must consider how you can apply this knowledge of the gangster movie to the question which is being asked. In a nutshell this is the key to developing a good response to genre questions on MED4.

Let's look at the first option on genre and audience expectations. Key words that you can use to regulate and structure your response are 'how' and 'why'. So your plan for this essay might revolve around those two words.

**How:**

Familiarity with texts of the same genre

Knowledge of codes and conventions, including narrative, character typology iconography

Familiarity with 'stars' of the genre

Marketing of text-based genre on appeal of familiarity

Guarantee of pleasure

Short cut to pleasure and understanding

Safe option

Ease of access

**Why:**

Guarantee of success in unpredictable market

Building on proven formula and formats

Industry geared up for repetition of established formats

Prepares and positions audience to be receptive to the text

Allows limited and controlled degrees of innovation

You can use these points as a checklist of ways into the questions, although you may not feel it necessary or appropriate to cover all of them. Although the question does not ask specifically for examples, you will no doubt realise that the front of the paper (see page 109) tells you that you should make 'specific reference to a range of media texts, contemporary and/or historical as appropriate'. So you need to consider how you might apply your knowledge of a genre you know well to the points jotted down above.

A good example might be soaps. So you can talk about:

Established range of available texts in the genre

Longevity of genre – *Coronation Street* from early 1960s

Established soap conventions – narrative devices and character typology

Stars and intertextuality – celebrity shows, and magazines and popular press

Trailing of texts and promotion in other media – *Inside Soap*

Audiences learn conventions and play with them, for example seeking to predict narrative outcomes

Giving pleasure

Safe – you know more or less you will get what it says on the tin

Reliable timings and slots on television

Long-running success of many soaps, therefore proven format

Industry invests heavily in sets and technology – Granada studios

Audience identifies with characters and storylines

Possible to innovate within the confines of established genre conventions

---

**ACTIVITY**

*Choose a couple of examples of soaps that you have studied and consider how you might use this knowledge of the texts to exemplify and support some of the points above*

*OR*

*Choose another genre with which you are familiar and devise an essay plan based on a similar set of points.*

---

The alternative question like so many in the section of MED4 states what is on the surface the blindingly obvious. There is a huge temptation to write: 'Of course genres must adapt in order to survive', and move on to the next question. Sadly although Principal Examiners can get away with stating the obvious, they are not prepared to reward candidates too highly for simply agreeing with them.

So what are you going to do with this question? The straightforward nature of the question and the imperative 'Discuss', should signal to you that this question is one that calls for you to rehearse a series of ideas linked to innovation within genre. Of course it also leaves you free to draw upon a range of different genres and their texts to expand upon and exemplify the points you wish to make.

It might be a good idea in an essay like this to define what you are talking about. So a simple statement as to what you believe genre to be might make a reasonable starting point. Of course, as soon as you attempt to define genre, you hit snags. On this occasion though the snags might be helpful because they should enable you to develop the idea that actually fixing the definition of an individual genre has always been a fraught business. Genres by their very nature evolve, change and develop. Genres are not static. How far they change and over what sort of time period is potentially part of the discussion.

Similarly there is also the opportunity to bring in some wider contexts at this point. What is it the drives innovation within genres? Is it the demands of the audience? Is it producers? Is it social and cultural forces? (That's right, all three.) Your discussion, however, can readily centre on how and why these factors influence genre but also some discussion is needed of the balance in this relationship. Which of the factors might most influence development within a genre? If you want to get really sophisticated in your response you might look at the balance between the factors too. The section above on reality TV might offer you some ideas of how to go about this.

Exemplification is absolutely necessary in a question of this sort. You are clearly being tested on your ability to take a fairly basic idea and show what you can do with it. Being able to pull out textual and contextual examples to support and illustrate your discussion is paramount.

In January 2005 the pair of genre questions on MED4 was as follows.

a **Are genre texts produced because their audiences are comfortable with the repetition of formulas?**

b **Is there a place for innovation within contemporary genre? Provide examples throughout your answer.**

**AQA January 2005**

Notice that both texts are framed on this occasion as questions. To both you might answer 'yes' or, rather more unlikely, 'no'. Of course you will be beginning to realise this is quite an interesting way of turning down the offer of a university place. In the end, 'yes' or 'no' does not really matter. The answer is about the quality of your argument and your ability to support and illustrate that argument. So you should be getting good at differentiating between two questions now. This means you will have figured out that the first question is focused on genre formulas and audiences whereas the second requires you to look at changes in genre today.

Let's look at (a). The answer 'yes' is certainly plausible, but needs the rider: but that's not the whole story. The reason that it is not the whole story you will surely know is that there is an argument that it is producers that are comfortable with the repetition of formulas as much, if not more so, than are audiences.

So what do you need to do with this question? Well a good idea is to kick off with the ideas around audiences and genre. So you need to go through some of the basic ideas of genre's appeal to audiences. You should have a good handle on these by now so it should be a straightforward job to rehearse them in a fairly concise manner. Look for around four key points.

Appeal of genre to audiences:

1

2

3

4

Next think about the issue of producers and genre. Why do they produce genre texts? Again these should be ideas that you are familiar with. So again make a list of key points. As before, around four should do it:

Appeal of genre to producers:

1

2

3

4

So there you have a skeletal plan of your essay. Into this you need to weave both exemplification and wider contexts. Exemplification should be pre-prepared at your fingertips for this type of predictable question. Wider contexts should allow you the opportunity to consider some of the social and cultural influences that might impact upon the appeal of a genre.

Finally note in this question the word 'repetition'. How accurate is it to describe what you see in the media as the repetition of formulas? There is also an argument to be had that talks about innovation within that repetition as in the June 2004 paper. So genre is about more than repetition you might argue.

There is a good chance that you will not find space in your response to include all of these points as well as exemplifying them. Be prepared to be selective and prioritise the points you feel you want to make. Given the open nature of this type of question, there is a degree of freedom in setting your own agenda. Be careful, however, not to stray too far from the prime focus of the question.

Question (b) again would benefit from some kind of upfront definition of genre and its function. It would also be a good idea to put your cards on the table and identify what you mean by 'innovation'. The focus of the question as you may well have gathered is about 'how' and 'why' there is innovation rather than simply whether there is any innovation at all.

As with the first question (and many other questions on genre yet to be asked by AQA) producers and audiences are going to be central to your answer. Perhaps the nuance that you should be exploring if you want to score a really high mark is the power balance between these two in the shaping of genre texts. Does innovation occur because audiences demand it tiring of the same old thing or is it driven by producers wanting to appear one step ahead of the game but still wishing to preserve the same tested formulas that have become embedded into their industrial processes?

In terms of wider contexts, there is an interesting argument to rehearse that looks at how social and cultural forces can be seen to drive innovation in specific genres. As we have seen media texts can be said to be a barometer reflecting the values and concerns of our culture. Clearly any shift in these values is going to impact the way texts are produced. Exploring how this happens and how texts are influenced is potentially a worthwhile focus in your study of genre. A straightforward example might be the way in which soap operas tackle issues such as teenage pregnancy, rape and drug abuse, as a reflection of broader social concerns about these issues.

# MEDIA AUDIENCES

This topic area has more demands specified than any of the others and perusing the list you will see that they are very wide ranging:

- Textual representations of audiences and the public

- Economic, social and political issues raised by the role of audiences

- Segmentation of audiences

- Theories of audience

- Political, social and economic functions of audiences

- Audience power

- Influence of new technologies

Don't be put off by this though, Audience must surely be the most important media concept and studying audience for MED4 will allow you to do some really dynamic and exciting work.

It is likely that you studied the ways audiences are segmented by media producers as part of your AS course, perhaps also theories of audience. At any rate, it will be easy to 'mug up' on these using the *Essential Introduction* books at AS and A2.

Audiences are segmented in the media industry chiefly as a convenience for marketing media products and selling audiences to advertisers.

The crudest tools for segmenting audience are perhaps demographic ones: gender, age and social class for example. Despite the increasing feeling that demographic variables constitute a rather blunt instrument there is good reason to argue for their continuing relevance. Many media texts are consumed along fairly strict gender lines and although it might be argued that a consideration of life stages is more meaningful than bald age differentiators it remains broadly true that people pursue set goals at predictable ages.

The pre-eminence of demographic variables as a tool of audience segmentation was supplanted by a more attitudinal approach characterised by Young and Rubicam. Here, shared values and beliefs pull rank in terms of identifying a discrete group.

Behavioural variables are also increasingly taken into consideration with many organisations using loyalty card schemes to develop more sophisticated profiles of their customers' habits and preferences, partly so that they can sell this information on to other interested parties.

Certainly media industries still spend vast amounts on collecting data about who is consuming their products, but one could argue that approaches to defining audiences are changing.

With the advent of digitalisation and the consequent reduction in production costs it has become possible in many media industries to break even while appealing to relatively small, highly specific niche audiences.

Many media organisations now offer potential advertisers profiles of a hypothetical typical consumer which is highly individualised. As we will learn later in the chapter, the power of audiences to avoid traditional advertising is increasing and advertisers are having to find new ways to impact upon their target group.

Furthermore, in the digital age with massively increased capacity for product (media texts) but a static audience niche advertising is increasingly the order of the day. This is one reason why studying audience behaviour has become so important. The advertiser may find it helpful to know that the target group are heavy Internet users rather than that they are male ABC1 30–40 year olds.

It is becoming relatively easy to access fairly detailed information about audience profiling via various media organisations that are funded by advertising.

A traditional approach to audience profiling:
www.condenastmediakit.com

And a more contemporary approach involving a more individualised profile:
www.futurenet.com/futureonline/adservices

You need to register to access this information and also have a pdf reader but it's worth it.

www.ipcmedia.com/magazines/
The best of the bunch. Choose a magazine title from the right-hand side. When the page loads click on 'download media information'. You need a pdf reader.

At A2 what is required is that you show you can apply these concepts and develop a critical response to them.

For example:

**'Audience segmentation is essential to deliver audiences to advertisers.' Discuss.**

**AQA June 2004**

Your knowledge of the segmentation methods is assumed. What's at issue here is the use to which they are put, their current relevance and applicability.

**4 b 'As we no longer see the audience as an undifferentiated mass, audience theories can be of little use.' Discuss.**

**AQA June 2005**

Again, there is an assumption here that you will be familiar with a range of audience theories and able to rehearse their relative usefulness. The term 'undifferentiated mass' glances back to early Effects Theory, but again the expectation seems to be that you can pick up this term and run with it, applying it to other theoretical perspectives.

Audience theories can be broken down into three main groups as the diagram on page 93 demonstrates.

Text-based theories were the first to develop and are often seen as the most out-of-date.

Yet it remains clear that media texts do affect people in one way or another. Our laughter or revulsion is an effect; imitation of sketch show catchphrases is another. The notion of the television watershed, whereby viewing after 9pm becomes the adult's rather than the broadcaster's responsibility, or the system of film classification are both underpinned by Effects Theory.

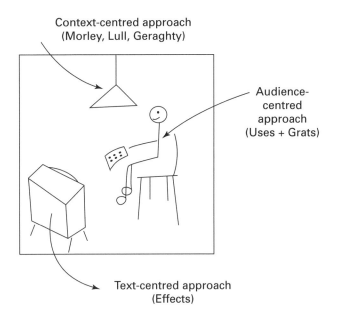

Context-centred approach
(Morley, Lull, Geraghty)

Audience-centred approach
(Uses + Grats)

Text-centred approach
(Effects)

**Figure 4**

Source: Morley, D. *The 'Nationwide' Audience: Structure and decoding* (1980), London, BFI; Lull, J. *Media Communication Culture: A global approach* (1995), Colombia University Press; Geraghty, C. *Women and Soap Operas* (1990), Oxford, Polity Press.

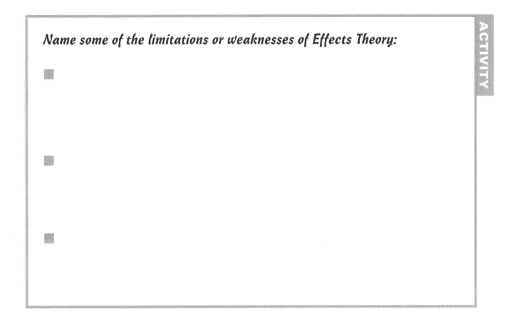

ACTIVITY

*Name some of the limitations or weaknesses of Effects Theory:*

■

■

■

Uses and Gratifications Theory puts the user or audience at the centre of the theory and offers us a model of a viewer who is in control of their media consumption and makes motivated choices about what they consume based on the needs they want fulfilled by the media.

ACTIVITY

*Name the four main uses and gratifications of TV identified by Blulmer and Katz (The Use of Mass Communication: Current Perspectives on Gratifications Research, Sage, 1975).*

- ■

- ■

- ■

- ■

But it is consumption theories that have more recently been in the ascendancy. This group of theories considers that the context in which the text is consumed will have a fundamental impact on the way in which it is interpreted. So we are concerned not only with the producer's 'preferred reading' but with other 'alternative' readings of different audience members. At the heart of Consumption Theory is the notion of differentiated interpretations. Here texts don't have fixed meanings – the meaning is determined by the consumer who brings his/her own subjective perceptions to the text.

In both cases – audience segmentation and audience theories – it can be seen that in industrial and academic contexts various tools for conceptualising about audiences have developed. These tools might be considered to be of variable use-fulness and the discussion required in exam answers is likely to revolve around this variability.

At A2 you are not simply showing you understand the terms of the question but are interpreting it and making individual choices about the directions in which you choose to pursue it. This sounds like a confident student!

Such confidence, of course, comes from a familiarity with the course content, the relevant theories and with planning and writing exam answers. Helpful too can be involvement in class discussions whereby you challenge others' perceptions and respond to challenges to your own ideas! Autonomy and authority in writing about your own media consumption is another key differentiator in answers at A2.

The issue of textual representations of audiences probably finds its natural home in discussing reality television shows, though as the specification indicates there are other ways into the issue.

In the earlier days of television the ways in which the audience were allowed on to the screen were very restricted and specific. Cutaways to the audience in quiz shows were important to generate atmosphere in the studio. Some game show formats drew participants from a studio audience so the audience becomes integral in that way, e.g. *The Price Is Right*. Light entertainment and variety shows have often relied on the presence of a studio audience for much of the show's content. Presenters such as Michael Barrymore, Cilla Black, Chris Evans and more recently Graham Norton and Ant and Dec have been associated with such forms of audience participation. Invariably such shows tended to be pitched to mainstream, lower class audiences, most usually screened on ITV during prime time. 'Ordinary people', representations of the audience in a sense, have always appeared in documentaries and news programmes and perhaps help the audience to see media content as a reflection of their lives and concerns.

With the advent of satellite, cable and digital television and the consequent explo-sion in programme capacity, the relationship between the audience and the programme changed. The imperative to make cheap programmes in volume received an unprecedented impetus, with a static audience fragmenting across an ever-widening range of viewing choices.

One way in which the industry sought to solve this problem was to make the audience the star. Confessional shows imported from the USA such as *Oprah*, *Jerry Springer* and *Ricki Lake* spawned a host of UK imitations such as *Trisha* and *Kilroy* where the studio audience become the content of the programme itself.

Investigative documentaries featuring journalists and expert witnesses were replaced by docu-soaps tracking members of the public in everyday tasks such as learning to drive (*Driving School*) or coping with domestic chores and child care (*Wife Swap*) using fly-on-the-wall techniques. This has the advantage not only of providing cheap content – no paid actors, no studio sets – but also adds relevance and frisson for the audience in seeing representations of themselves against which they can evaluate their own identity and status.

Reality television seemed to become an addiction for both audiences and institutions and an increasing range of generic hybrids featuring 'ordinary people' evolved. Shows such as *Big Brother* combine game show and documentary elements to offer an unprecedentedly close look at how people operate in a pressure-cooker environment. The press has repeatedly vilified reality television as dumbed down entertainment and boring but many of the shows continue to be ratings winners. In Autumn 2005 the BBC revived the popular *What Not To Wear* series. The new series was billed as featuring divorced women, rather than, as most recently, using celebrities. The trailer showed the dozens of videos sent to the show by women hoping to feature on it.

Another important dimension of the textual representation of audiences is that created through the increased interactive content of many contemporary media texts. The rather archaic phone-in is still a staple of many radio shows, though in part it has perhaps been superseded by texting and emailing. It is interesting to note just how much of the content of independent radio stations is based on input or feedback from the listening audience. On the Galaxy breakfast show for example, traditional competition responses ('What's That Noise?', 'Hook, Line and Stinker', 'How High?') jostle alongside requests for songs and comments about the music played as well as information provided by the audience about local traffic problems. In addition to this comments are invited about some rather puerile topic of the day, for example, 'tell us about your friends that smell' or 'texts that went wrong' and the audience are invited to vote in a range of impromptu polls. Some BBC radio stations also depend upon audience input to enliven otherwise rather dry and serious news and sport. The rather high-brow Radio 4 tends not to promote interactivity but the more mainstream and populist Radio 5 makes frequent and regular requests for comments and opinions on both news and sporting matters. On television too, the notion of audience consumption as a two-way process is to be seen everywhere.

*Think of five different ways in which audiences interact with contemporary television programmes.*

- ▪
- ▪
- ▪
- ▪
- ▪

An increasing number of shows rely on text voting by the audience to propel the narrative forward. Game shows with elimination formats such as *Strictly Come Dancing* and *X Factor* rely on audience interaction to produce the line-up for the next episode. This investment in the show not only accrues revenue through the cost of the calls, but also helps to guarantee a future audience by creating a drama around who 'survives' into the next round. The audience is thereby given the illusion of empowerment and the traditional line between the active producer and passive audience is blurred.

The notion of the audience as producer is one which the digital network has exploited to the full. Increased capacity and digitally compressed content gives much greater scope for audience viewing options within any given show. For example, Sky News offers a service called 'Sky News Active' accessed by digital customers through the red button. This service enables viewers to select news in one of any eight categories at the touch of a button. The screen also divides into different segments to access a variety of news simultaneously by different methods: visually, graphically by selecting information from a menu or even by selecting ticker tape options to run across the bottom of the screen. Other interactive features include the invitation to vote on a selection of news topics of the day. Many of these are suitably populist to meet the needs of the target audience, for example, 'Will Daniel Craig make a good James Bond?'

A similar array of options greets the sports fan on Sky. When a live football match is aired, for example, the red button allows the viewer to access a choice of camera angles, commentary modes and to track the moves of a specific player. In addition the player can opt to view the highlights of that game up to the current point in the match at any time. The ability to choose different audio options is a particularly interesting one from the fan's point of view. Most football fans consider themselves pundits and many bemoan the commentary that is traditionally overlaid on the action. The option to choose only crowd sound attempts to replicate a live game scenario, whereas the chance to select fan commentary exposes the viewer to the excesses of partisan, man-down-the-pub opinion.

Hopefully, what becomes clear is that the television-watching experience is thereby transformed from passive and subordinate to much more active and empowered. At least, this is the hype that the manufacturers of digital television would like us to buy into. But is viewer power real or illusory?

| ACTIVITY | *Identify arguments for and against the view that digitalisation has delivered the audience greater power:* |
|---|---|

| *FOR* | *AGAINST* |
|---|---|
| ■ | ■ |

| FOR | AGAINST |
|-----|---------|
| ■ | ■ |
| ■ | ■ |
| ■ | ■ |
| ■ | ■ |

One piece of hardware that helps us to answer this question and really does threaten to revolutionise the way we watch television is the personalised video recorder. You may know this product under its trade names Sky+ or TiVo. The equipment basically does the same job as a DVD recorder or VCR but stores programmes as digital files for replay or download to disk or tape.

On the face of it this seems a fairly unassuming piece of kit and sales have been rather slow to take off. Sky, for example, has been reduced to discounting the price of its hardware to existing customers and rolling-up the purchase of the hard drive recorder with other inducements, e.g. Sky Multi-Room.

On the other hand, the technology can deliver some impressive features: chief among these is probably pausing live television while you take a phone call or nip to the loo. The hard disk can store at least 30 hours of television and this figure is rising with each new product that comes onto the market. In so doing time-shifting programmes becomes not only a possibility but potentially a whole new way of watching television – indeed some personalised video recorders (PVRs) have been marketed as giving the viewer the chance to create their own television schedule.

In conjunction with digital television, which in any case approaches scheduling on the assumption that viewers pick-and-mix across channels at will, this does seem to deliver significantly greater self-determining power for the viewer. The ultimate test of the audience's autonomy, however, is the extent to which they can liberate themselves from television's paymasters: advertisers. One significant feature of PVR technology is its capacity for so-called 'ad-avoidance'. Audiences using 'skip' features can successfully navigate their way around all adverts, a development on the ubiquitous channel-flicking that many already use to ad-avoid.

No wonder the industry has had mixed feelings about this technology: you don't bite the hand that feeds you after all! Before you celebrate the ascendancy of the audience however a couple of points should be noted:

- Advertisers have been consoled by news that where PVRs are owned the hours spent watching television increases.

- As time-shifting becomes a way of life, broadcasters have argued to advertisers that all slots become 'prime' because an apparently graveyard slot can garner a much greater audience if time-shifting is taken into account.

- Furthermore, sponsorship of television programmes has become more lucrative on the grounds that the idents either side of ad breaks help viewers to navigate to their chosen material.

It is without question that technological developments offer audiences more choices and more control but it could be argued that for as long as this power is situated in a commercial context it is of necessity more illusory than real.

The key notion of economic, social and political contexts which underpins all of A2 is referred to twice in this topic area's specific demands. Usefully the specification explains that in terms of each context the audience can be viewed differently:

Political = audience as citizen

Social = audience as consumer

Economic = audience as product

Interestingly, this bears more than a passing resemblance to the different perspectives offered by audience theory (see above).

In the public service model the audience is 'educated' and informed'; they are 'improved' in order to enhance their citizenship. Such notions may appear very archaic, harking back as they do to Reithian concepts of education by stealth and a patrician broadcasting system that 'knows what's best' for its audience. However, it is still possible to see the best of these intentions enshrined in the BBC's continuing commitment to appeal to a broad audience, to inclusivity and to social improvement and audience empowerment. Arguably, digitalisation has given the BBC a new lease of life, giving it extra capacity to appeal to minority groups and pursue projects for highly niche audiences. BBCi, the Internet service, is another dimension of this continuing goal of education and information every bit as important as entertainment in its remit.

From a uses and gratifications perspective the audience is a consumer, making motivated choices about what they consume and for what purpose. This approach implies the audience is in full control of the choices it makes and that the choosing is from a repertoire representing real choice. It could easily be argued, however, with reference to more contemporary theories that this choosing is neither fully conscious nor meaningful, given that the menu is pre-determined by predominantly white male producers and that viewing takes place within a context of unequal power relations (who controls the remote?) and maybe a secondary or tertiary rather than a primary experience.

The most reductive approach to context is that which views the audience as no more than a product, delivered primarily to advertisers. It has long been argued that commercial television constructs an audience to be sold for the purposes of advertising. From this perspective the audience is a passive entity and the programme a conduit through which the audience are sweetened to consume adverts. The hypo-dermic model envisaged exactly such a scenario, where the audience subconsciously imbibes the influences to which it has been exposed. The fact that manufacturers continue to rate television advertising as a prime medium to reach their audiences should convince us of the validity of this approach. The connection between commerce and television is becoming ever more explicit and direct with shopping channels and the use of the television as a means to order pizza, book holidays and a myriad other paid-for functions, including of course pay-to-view. How long can it be before we can press the red button during adverts to buy the item we see?

So what view should we take about the status of the audience in the contemporary media dynamic?

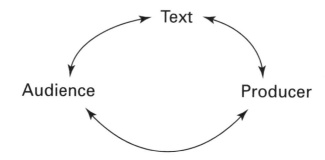

**Figure 5**

Has digitalisation finally begun to deliver a democratised media, hitherto denied audiences by patrician producers and institutions? Or has the audience become the ultimate victim of a dumbed-down media which in its increasing desperation to make a commercial profit has lost all sense of principle and responsibility? See the activity box opposite.

To end this section let's think a little more closely about the examination's demands.

For each topic area you have a choice of two questions and must answer one of them.

Look at past papers on www.aqa.org.uk and consider the differences between the two questions.

- Equal difficulty.
- Tests different aspects of the specification.
- Varying focus: broad or more directed.
- May be 'hung' on a quote.
- Require textual examples, even if this isn't explicit.

You need to attempt answers to different sorts of questions to see which suits you better. As a fail-safe work towards coping with your less-preferred style of question! Check you understand the terminology of the questions so that you don't feel uncertain about the appropriateness of your response.

*Identify arguments and textual examples to support each of the above positions and decide where your own views lie.*

| AUDIENCE EMPOWERED | AUDIENCE VICTIMISED |
|---|---|
| *Arguments* | *Arguments* |
| ■ | ■ |
| ■ | ■ |
| ■ | ■ |
| ■ | ■ |
| *Examples* | *Examples* |
| ■ | ■ |
| ■ | ■ |

*Write a power paragraph that summarises the two main perspectives, using examples, and outline your own personal view.*

You don't really want to be in a situation where you are forced to answer one question because you are unprepared for the topic material on the other. This is a particular danger with this topic area where the specific demands are so many and so wide-ranging – in practice though audience theories have been a popular focus, as have issues of audience participation. At any rate, bear in mind:

■ A range of theories and issues should be understood.

■ Some detailed knowledge will be needed.

■ Be prepared to apply that knowledge so that you use what you know to engage the examiner, construct an argument and generate some sort of debate.

Here's an example using a brainstorm and plan answer to a question from June 2004:

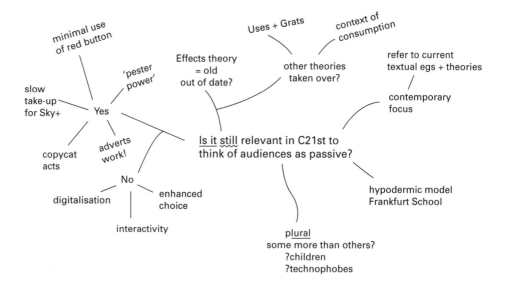

**Figure 6**

Break the question down and reflect on any issues arising:

■ A strong theoretical focus here . . . but don't forget the need for textual examples

■ 'Is it . . .' Yes AND no

■ 'Still' harks back to an old theory. Others taken over?

■ 'Relevant in twenty-first century' contemporary focus. Need up-to-date knowledge of theories. And practical textual examples.

■ 'Audiences' plural. Some more than others: children? Those with less power?

■ 'Passive' specific knowledge of Effects Theory. How the concept might relate to other theories.

Order the points from the spidergram making sure there are different and appropriate textual examples for each paragraph/point.

1   Variety of audience theories over decades, some arguing for audience's passivity, others not. Though Effects Theory has been 'supplanted' good reason for scepticism. Most recent theories stress an awareness of different contexts and situations and the effects this may have on an audience member's responses.

2   On the face of it the old Effects Theory idea of the hypodermic syringe seems an irrelevance in contemporary terms. Rehearse theory. Current examples including digitalisation leading to enhanced choice, interactivity, audience as scheduler, democratisation, blurring of line between consumer and producer.

3   Other theories have been and gone since Effects. Uses and Gratifications seemed more realistic with its notion of the audience making motivated choices on the basis of their needs . . . choosing to escape, to be informed, etc.

4   Yet there is plenty of evidence to support the view that audiences remain passive. Most viewers don't use the red button, even when they own it. Many pay for Sky channels but persist in watching terrestrial television predominantly. Concerns remain about appropriateness of television content, pester power, copycat acts – all underpinned by a notion of passive audiences uncritically absorbing television content.

5   Modern theories based in contexts of consumption stress the differential patterns of activity/passivity between different audience members. So the key may lie in the notion of 'audiences': some responding passively, others more actively and critically. For the more naïve and vulnerable, i.e. children or those with less control over the watching process e.g. women – no control of the remote and technophobic (stereotypically) – the notion of passivity remains highly relevant.

6   Conclusion. The answer lies in which audience is being considered. Though we allegedly live in the age of audience power – elimination votes, Sky+ etc. it

seems premature and naïve to presuppose that all audiences are making motivated, active choices about their media consumption. Their passivity may not itself be a problem but as media students we should recognise and acknowledge it.

Candidates taking the exam in June 2003 where confronted with the following questions on this topic:

a **Why are television shows that feature 'real people' so popular? Illustrate your answer with examples.**

b **How useful are audience theories in understanding media consumption? Discuss.**

**AQA June 2003**

It would be harder to imagine questions that ask for two such seemingly different responses at least at first glance. With any luck you will be alive to what is a great big trap door in question (a). If not you will waltz into the exam room and see this as your big chance to tell the examiner why you love/hate or are indifferent to reality television. Beware the general studies answer. If you hear yourself sounding like the loudmouth down the pub, you are wide of the mark on this one.

So how do you turn such a potentially open question into a display of your knowledge of all things about audience theory? Well realise in this question that you may have to go some way beyond the confines of traditional audience theory. If you have gone into the exam and the only thing you know is the Frankfurt School, and so on then look at the other question. This question is very much about the application of audience theory. What do theories of audience tell us about audience behaviour and specifically what they like and dislike.

We suggested as an approach to writing essay putting everything that you think might be relevant down onto a sheet of the answer book. Here is the sort of thing you might come up with for this question:

- Focus on audience participation
- Performers are the audience or at least their representatives
- Voting and interaction
- Empowering audiences – shaping narrative
- Digitalisation, interactivity, convergence

- Voyeuristic appeal of reality television

- Surveillance

- Life in a virtual community

You have in this list a combination of uses and gratifications, the relationship between audience and producer, and technological innovation. Central to all of this is the idea of audiences exerting power over the texts they consume and by implication the institutions that produce them. In terms of wider contexts you might well wish to explore the extent to which this is 'real' power and how much it is simply contrived to swell audiences and to raise revenue from phone calls and texts.

Be alert throughout your answer to a question like this that there is an ongoing danger of losing focus. You should be at pains throughout to bring your answer back to the issue of audience.

In question (b) you are asked to assess the value of audience theories. Given that this is potentially a lifetime's study, this question is potentially a pretty tall order. Remember that examiners are expected 45 minutes of focused response – not a lifetime's study. You need to decide at a very early stage where to take this essay. A list of all the theories you know is not a way to get a good mark, although it would probably get you through the exam if you did it in sufficient detail. Your job is to evaluate. That means first showing that you know the major theories and then making your assessment of their usefulness.

So job number one is to decide what you consider to be the key theories here. Try writing your own list or if you want to be lazy look at the one above generated for the June 2004 paper. Note the movement from passive to active in terms of audience theory. How far you think this is true might be a good question to ask. It seems a bit of received wisdom in Media Studies that audiences have got more clever, but have they? If they have how do you account for the popularity of:

- Jordan and Peter

- Simon Cowell

- Ant and Dec

Think about the fact the audience theory is limited because of the complexity of what it is dealing with. Audiences are composed of individuals who do not behave as a homogenous mass. Just check around your family and friends and the variety of response to media texts they will have. If audience behaviour could be predicted, film producers would never produce an expensive turkey.

You might also like to think about how technology has influenced the way we think about audiences and determined the ways in which they behave. Much audience study was undertaken before the decline of the mass audiences and the arrival of segmented audiences and interactivity through digitalisation and convergence technology.

Similarly you might explore how from a theoretical perspective postmodern approaches to Media Studies might see audiences as having a more playful approach to media texts, appropriating them for their own uses. This is clearly a long way from the hypodermic model.

General Certificate of Education
June 2005
Advanced Level Examination

> Title of the paper. Make sure you are in the right exam.

**MEDIA STUDIES**
**Unit 4    Texts and Contexts in the Media**

**MED4**

> Date and time of the exam. You should know this well in advance. Make sure you arrive in plenty of time.

Monday 20 June 2005  Afternoon Session

**In addition to this paper you will require:**
an 8-page answer book.

> If you need more sheets, ask for them. Don't forget to put your name and number on each one.

Time allowed: 1 hour 30 minutes

> So forty minutes a question plus ten minutes reading, planning and checking. The pressure is on!

**Instructions**

> Don't forget to bring one that works and a spare in case it doesn't.

- Use blue or black ink or ball-point pen.
- Write the information required on the front of your answer book. The *Examining Body* for this paper is AQA. The *Paper Reference* is MED4.
- Answer **two** questions. Each question must be taken from a different section.

> No marks for this unfortunately.

**Information**

> Got it?     So equal time on each.

- The maximum mark for this paper is 60. All questions carry 30 marks.
- In this paper you will be expected to:

> These are a simplified version of the assessment objectives. This is what MED4 is all about. Don't ignore this!

  – show the influence of wider contexts on contemporary and historical media texts
  – comment on and evaluate media theories, debates, ideas and information
  – show what you know about media texts and ideas using the Key Concepts.

> So sound enthusiastic and knowledgeable (engaged) and show you know lots of relevant texts, mostly contemporary.

- You will be rewarded for:
  – your personal engagement with media texts
  – specific reference to a range of media texts, contemporary and/or historical, as appropriate.
- You are reminded of the need for good English and clear presentation. Your answers should be in continuous prose. Quality of written communication will be assessed.

> So write clearly and legibly. Organise your answers. Be as careful as you can with spelling, punctuation and grammar. Above all use the terminology you have learned that is specific to Media Studies.

# 110

## SAMPLE MARK SCHEME FOR THE AQA A2 MEDIA STUDIES MED4 EXAMINATION WITH AN EXPLANATION OF HOW IT CAN HELP YOU

The mark scheme for MED4 is generic which means with the odd word or two changed, the mark scheme for all questions is basically the same. This is the top level mark band for question 1(a) but the comments might apply equally to any of the questions on MED4. Candidates who do these things will get a mark of between 26–30.

Means that you talk about things that are relevant and you do so with assurance that comes from knowing what you are talking about.

Advanced – *Media Studies*

Mark Scheme

### Question 1(a)

**(30 marks)**

What you write is well structured, logical and makes sense.

You refer to lots of contexts that impact on texts.

**Discuss the impact of recent changes in the production and presentation of news.**

**Level 6 (26-30 marks)**

You give lots of examples.

These examples show you know the theories and issues relevant to this topic.

The answer shows confident and appropriate discussion, references a wide range of contextual influences and provides detailed illustration which demonstrates a comprehensive knowledge and understanding of current ideas, theories, debates or information about recent changes in the production and presentation of news. An engaged response, clearly organised and presented, with detailed and appropriate exemplification.

**Level 5 (21-25 marks)**

You use examples that fit in with what you are saying.

It is you talking, not your teacher, and you have got involved with the topic using media concepts and terminology.

The answer shows competent and appropriate personal discussion, references a wide range of contextual influences and provides competent illustration which demonstrates proficient knowledge and understanding of current ideas, theories, debates or information about recent changes in the production and presentation of news. An engaged personal response, well organised and presented, with competent and appropriate exemplification.

**Level 4 (16-20 marks)**

The answer shows sound personal discussion, references a range of contextual influences and provides sound illustration which demonstrates solid knowledge and understanding of current ideas, theories, debates or information about recent changes in the production and presentation of news. A generally sound personal response, competently organised and presented, with sound exemplification.

**Level 3 (11-15 marks)**

The answer shows some personal discussion based on a consideration of contextual factors and provides some illustration which demonstrates sketchy knowledge and understanding of current ideas, theories, debates or information about recent changes in the production and presentation of news. A simple personal response, competently organised with some relevant exemplification.

**Level 2 (6-10 marks)**

Illustration is basic with little or no knowledge or understanding of current ideas, theories, debates or information about recent changes in the production and presentation of news. A superficial and/or confused response with little relevant exemplification.

**Level 1 (0-5 marks)**

There may be one or two isolated points of some relevance such as some knowledge or application of Key Concepts, any attempt to answer the question or any exemplification. The answer shows next to no awareness of any ideas, theories, debates or information about recent changes in the production and presentation of news.

# PART 2

# COMPARATIVE CRITICAL ANALYSIS (MED6)

## INTRODUCTION

When you first see what you have to do for the MED6 exam, you can be forgiven for thinking that you are seeing double. Having already demonstrated that you are adept at analysing a media text in the MED1 AS, you might think it is a bit pointless now analysing two. In some ways you are right, but as AQA has seen fit to ask you to jump a hurdle very similar to one you have already cleared, then it would be foolish to complain at what appears to be a relatively good piece of fortune.

Before you get carried away though, let's take a careful look at what MED6 is actually all about. We also need to bear in mind those twin principles that inform our A2 study, wider contexts and theoretical debates.

A good place to start is with the exam paper itself. What exactly is the task set for you on the paper? Here is what the June 2005 paper required.

> **Using the comparison of these two texts as your starting point, explore the media issues and debates which they raise. In your answer you will need to address:**
>
> ■ **Key Concepts**
>
> ■ **Contextual factors**
>
> ■ **Media theory** AQA June 2005

What you will not have noticed is that there has been a change in the wording from that which appeared on papers prior to 2005. When exam boards change wordings on papers it sometimes signals a change in the approach they are taking to the assessment of particular units. The change in this case is in the emphasis placed on what you are expected to do with this task. Rather than provide a simple comparison of the two texts identifying similarities and differences as candidates had previously been asked to do, the revamped question demands an exploration that will take you into looking at both wider contexts and theoretical issues.

So a simple model for approaching this paper might take the following form:

Comparison of two texts

Theoretical issues they raise

Wider contexts they suggest

NOTE

MED6 is an example of an assessment phenomenon created when A levels were revised in 2000 which is known as synopticity. It is in fact a synoptic paper. The word 'synoptic' relates to synopsis which describes a summary of the whole of something, often quite extensive. So the word is used here in the sense of drawing together different strands of what you have learned in the other units, including the AS units. One key idea behind the paper is that you will use all of the knowledge and skills you have acquired previously on your course to help you deal with this comparative textual analysis. So clearly something much more is demanded of you than simply repeating the approach that you adopted to MED1, Reading the Media.

Enough of all this background stuff – you want to know how to pass the MED6 exam. Well let's go back to the model we suggested above.

## TEXTS

You obviously need to start by engaging with the texts. This is an unseen exam so the texts will very likely be unknown to you. They may even be in a media form that you have little familiarity with. The only limitation as to what can be used is that the texts in some way can be classified as mass media and that they are in such a form that they can be made available in an exam room, i.e. print, video or sound, although the latter has so far not been used. The paper advises you to spend 30 minutes considering the text before you start writing your answer. As with MED1 you can take notes. If one or both of the texts is in video format, you will obviously need to watch it carefully and get some detailed notes as you won't have it available for reference once the screening is over.

Both texts of course do not have to be in the same media form. It is quite possible that a print text and a moving image text can be juxtaposed for you to tackle. So you really do need to be ready for anything in this exam.

NOTE

Mark schemes: just as the MED6 paper was revamped, so was the mark scheme. Here is what an examiner is looking for in the top level of the MED6 mark scheme. This is what you need to do in order to score between 51 and 60 marks.

NOTE

Candidates need to make extensive use of their learning at AS and A2 levels in responding to the texts, with sophisticated knowledge and application of wider contexts relevant to the materials.

Candidates need to show very good evidence of critical autonomy – the ability to make individual judgements informed by relevant theories, issues and debates.

Candidates need to demonstrate evidence of very good synoptic ability (drawing together theories, issues and debates from different parts of the specification) in making effective textual readings and comparisons based on a comprehensive understanding and application of all relevant key concepts.

Candidates need to show a sophisticated identification of the similarities and differences between the two texts, in a well structured and engaged response showing a very clear understanding of the form and function of the different materials.

So you need to:

- Show off what you have learned in two years of Media Studies
- Show you are independent in your thinking in using theories, etc. to write about the texts
- Show you have seen your media course as a whole and can pull together the threads of it
- See the similarities and differences in the texts and wrap the whole bit up in a well-wrought essay.

That's all!

## CONNECTIONS

So what might you look for when you first get the chance to look at the texts that have been chosen? Well obviously you need to figure out what links the two together. This might for example be the theme that they are dealing with. It may be that both texts deal with some aspect of reality television or refer to films of a similar genre. The link may be quite obvious or it may be a little more tenuous.

Similarly the link may not be so much thematic as to do with the form or genre of the texts. For example you may have two advertisements for different products perhaps using similar techniques or even very different techniques. Whatever you managed to identify as links, in terms of similarities and differences, is going to have an important bearing on where you go from here.

## WIDER CONTEXTS

Now this is the tricky bit in an unseen exam. As with any exam there is an element of luck involved here. It may be the texts are something that you know a lot about, perhaps even something you have worked on in your MED5 study. Equally it may be an area of the media that you have had little involvement with and you may feel initially a bit at sea with it. Remember that examiners cannot expect you to know a lot about specific texts you have never seen before. They can however expect you to show that you are familiar with the nature of media texts and that you have the deductive skills to make interpretations about the wider contexts from the texts themselves. For example an extract from a news bulletin may well be talking about a news event with which you are unfamiliar. What you are, or should be, familiar with are:

1    The nature of news bulletins

2    How stories are covered

From this you can deduce an awful lot about the specific story you have been asked to deal with. You will also be able to say something about the different nature of news broadcasts on different channels on television with any luck. You might even be able to consider the role of news bulletins in terms of the scheduling of television programmes. So immediately you can see that in many ways the wider contexts are implicit within the texts that you will have been presented with.

## ISSUES RAISED

We have already been hinting at some of these in our exploration of wider contexts. Remember the phrasing of the question is about using the comparison of these texts as a starting point. This means that you have the opportunity to explore any appropriate issue that you feel is raised by the texts. To some extent you are being asked to set your own agenda in relation to how you tackle this question. Perhaps, though, a word of caution is needed. This is not intended to be an opportunity for you to write any essay you choose. A good response will do at least two things:

1   Keep referring back to the texts to support and clarify any argument or proposition that is being put forward.

2   Keep some kind of balanced overview of the topic signalled by the text.

For example, if you are confronted with two extracts from news bulletins, then it would be easy to be tempted to want to focus on an issue like objectivity in television news coverage. This is fine as long as you are also going to consider other issues, for example presentational styles in television news that the extracts might have signalled. While MED6 is to a large extent about showcasing what you have learned in your two years of Media Studies it still imposes on you the constraints of focusing on the task common to all externally set examinations.

## THEORETICAL PERSPECTIVES

As we pointed out earlier in the book, theoretical perspectives are what distinguishes a study of the media from informed opinion that you might get from the population as a whole. Remember too that this is a synoptic unit and one therefore that you need to show that you have grasped some of the key theoretical issues that underpin a study of the media. The worst thing you can do, however, is to throw in theories in a contrived and inappropriate manner. On no account should you go into the exam with a couple of theories ready to use regardless of the texts that are set.

The theories that you choose to employ need to be relevant to the texts that you are exploring. If they are not, you will get precious little reward for introducing them. In the examination of two news bulletins, it would obviously be appropriate to look at some of the theoretical issues that relate to news gathering, news agendas and the presentation of news. If you have done any reading around news as a topic area, then you will be able to draw upon some of these theoretical ideas about the aspects of news to help support your arguments. Additionally some audience theory about the uses that audiences have for news would show a good level of engagement with Media Studies. You might also have recourse to some of the perspectives in the list on page 8. For example a feminist perspective might interpret news as being a patriarchal interpretation of the world serving the need to maintain the power of men in our social order. A Marxist perspective might similarly identify a news bulletin as a text doing the ideological work of preserving the power of the ruling elite.

NOTE

One question that you may have asked yourself is about referencing in exams. If you have done a decent job of your MED5 coursework, then you will have learned to reference properly by acknowledging ideas and quotations from previously published sources. Of course this is not practical in an exam where you are writing against the clock and do not have access to the necessary books to give the reference. It is likely however that you will know the names of major theorists who have published articles and books on media topics. Wherever possible use their names as a means of attributing the idea to them. This not only gives your essay authority and authenticity, it also does a great deal to show how you have immersed yourself in the discipline of Media Studies.

So for example, you may write: 'As Noam Chomsky points out the more you can increase fear of drugs and crime, welfare mothers, immigrants and aliens, the more you control all the people.'

Of course it is vitally important that you ensure that you are quoting the right person. Getting it wrong will make you look more stupid than not knowing it at all.

ACTIVITY

*In your notes try to get down a page of quotes from theorists and commentators you might be able to use in response to MED6 texts. Don't bother to learn the quotes word perfect. Just make sure that you can summarise the idea in a single sentence. Make sure too that you understand exactly what it means.*

It is a good idea to write down some kind of template for your answer as soon as you go into the exam. Many candidates write down some kind of acronym for the key concepts at the beginning of their notes. This is not really a helpful idea. If by this stage of the course you are still stuck trying to remember the key concepts, it might be a good idea to study something else. It is an equally bad idea to prompt yourself into any kind of mechanistic approach to this exam. Being successful is about being able to think on your feet. Good answers are fresh and engaged responses to the text, not mechanical regurgitation of learned and inappropriate formulas for dealing with the exam. So no 'MIGRAIN' please. Better a simple framework that allows you freedom to explore the texts in a controlled but open ended manner such as:

Texts

Connections

Wider contexts

Issues raised

Theoretical perspectives

## GETTING DOWN TO IT

The MED6 exam lasts for one and a half hours. Thirty minutes of this time is intended for reading and/or viewing of the texts. As with MED1, if the text is recorded on video this will be played to you three times over a period of 15 minutes with breaks in between. In general the length of moving image texts is restricted to around six minutes in order to allow plenty of time for candidates to make notes in response to what they have seen. Where there are two video texts, you clearly need to get down some detailed notes to refer to throughout the exam. If one or more of the texts are print based you will have these to refer to throughout the exam so the pressure to get down information about the texts will not be quite so compelling.

The specification and the exam paper recommend that you spend 30 minutes at the beginning of the exam considering the texts and making notes. Examiners are instructed not to mark any of your notes so from the point of view of how you are assessed it does not matter too much what you write. Of course from the point of view of the subsequent essay you produce, it matters a good deal what you write.

**NOTE**

Be certain to ensure that you make it clear which bit of your script is the written answer and which is notes. Draw a line clearly under your notes and then cross through them with a diagonal line so that the examiner knows immediately what to mark and what not to mark.

There is a wide range of approaches to writing your notes. Provided they make sense and help you write a good answer you should feel free to adopt the style that suits you best. What you do need to take account of is the fact that you may well be hit with a rush of random thoughts as soon as you have had a chance to digest the texts presented to you. A lot of these thoughts will be really valuable. Some of them will be pure rubbish. There is a lot to be said for getting them down regardless at this initial stage. Discriminating and sorting the good from the bad can come later. You will probably find that some very good ideas come out of these first reactions, so it is a good idea to hold on to them.

With any luck, your second wave of ideas will be a little more controlled and considered. Some will be new ideas; many will be refinements and developments of the first wave. At this stage it is a good idea to try to give shape to some of these ideas by considering the headings we have above. So you should be having ideas which:

■ identify links and common ground between the texts

■ suggest some of the wider contexts that are relevant to a consideration of the two texts

■ focus on some of the issues that you think are raised by the text from a Media Studies perspective

■ consider how you might apply some specific theoretical perspectives to the texts and the issues they raise.

It may be that your ideas will fall neatly into place and you can tuck them under these headings, but chances are they won't. What you may end up with is a series of points scattered across the pages of your answer booklet that don't really connect well at all. At this stage that is not a problem. It is better to use your adrenalin to get down plenty of ideas than it is to try to pigeonhole ideas into some kind of neat filing system.

> The standard eight-page answer book issued for taking exams has an irritating dozen or so lines at the bottom of the front page. It is all the space there is room for after your candidate details have been filled in. It is a good idea to ignore this space and turn over. You now have a large double page on which to get down your notes. As long as you do not write in the margin – a grievous crime in examining circles – you are free to use this big space to get down you ideas.
>
> NOTE

Once you feel that you have got down all the notes you feel you need, it is time to start working on them to give your essay a shape. A good exam response is ordered and logical. It consists of paragraphs that take you from one point to the next to build up into a meaningful sequence of ideas. In exam terms the paragraph is the cornerstone of any good essay-style response. If ever you find yourself writing a whole MED6 answer in one paragraph, you either did not write very much, or what you did write is likely to be pretty garbled. Try to think around three paragraphs to each page of an answer book as a rule of thumb.

So getting back to your notes. The first job is to fence off any you think are wide of the mark or perhaps rather less significant than you initially thought. Put a box of some sort round them. Don't cross them out; you might need them later. Next look for connection in your notes. By this we mean points that will link logically together. So for example in a comparison of two news items you might want to make the point that one news item appears to have a higher priority than another. This point would link well into a paragraph in which you are looking at the wider issue and theoretical perspective that relate to how news stories are prioritised and how the priorities may vary according to the context in which a bulletin is broadcast and consumed. Notice here that you are yourself making a complex connection between the texts, wider contexts and the theoretical perspectives.

> **NOTE**
>
> The ability to write an essay response that demonstrates an ability to link complex points and ideas is always the sign of a confident and well-prepared candidate. The reason for making notes is to provide you with the raw materials for your answer. A good essay response will take these raw materials and transform them into a coherent, rational and persuasive argument, an achievement always highly rewarded by examiners.

In fact the more able you are to interlink points into a coherent argument, the better you are likely to score. It should be the mark of an A2 student that s/he is able to put forward their ideas in a way that has moved on from a simplistic listing of 'key' points, often going little beyond the key concepts. This is one of the reasons that acronyms like MIGRAIN actually prevent students from achieving rather than in fact helping them to do so. You can just about get away with this kind of formulaic response at AS, although it is not to be recommended. At A2 examiners expect a much greater degree of sophistication. After all you have been studying the media for the best part of two years if not more.

> **ACTIVITY**
>
> *We have used as a reference point a comparison of two texts based on extracts from television news bulletins. At the time of writing no such texts have been set for MED6. It would, however, provide some useful practice*

*to consider how you might tackle one. You can get started by choosing a couple of extracts yourself. You will need to record them onto DVD or video for reference. Choose something like the opening of an early evening news programme on BBC1 and a similar extract from a later bulletin on Sky News. Alternatively you might like to look at two more contrasting examples such as BBC3 Sixty Seconds and part of BBC2 Newsnight. Don't worry about the precise timings of the extracts, but do avoid making them too long as you may simply have too much material.*

OK, so now have a go at following the strategy outlined above. Watch the extracts and start making some notes. Here are some cues that might prompt you.

Similarities/differences in texts – presentational styles, studio, presenters, music, introduction, graphics, running order of stories, use of location reporters, amount of video footage/studio shots.

Wider contexts. Broadcast slot, channel, how audience is addressed, role of technology in presenting news. Nature of news presenters.

Theoretical perspective. Role and function of television new bulletins. News sources, agendas and priorities. Sources of news. Ideological function of news bulletins. Objectivity and bias in news presentation. Audiences and news.

Issues raised: what are the key issues that you would want to tease out of the above?

MED6 as you can probably see is something of a wildcard as far as A2 exams are concerned. You can never be at all sure of what is going to come up in the exam. This makes preparation difficult in comparison to MED4 which gives you at least some opportunity to have texts prepared and ready for use in the exam. Don't use this as a cop out though. There is still a lot that you can do by way of preparation so don't fool yourself or lull yourself into some false sense of security about the exam.

As we have suggested previously, MED6 is in part about making connections. One useful thing you can be doing by way of preparation is practising seeing links between texts. These links are everywhere, not least because it is part of the postmodern condition of the media that it is hugely self-referential and feeds off itself at every opportunity. So consider the reporting of reality television shows and soap operas in the popular press. Look for headlines in the *Sun* and *Mirror* about the real and imaginary events surrounding the lives of the stars of these programmes.

Consider the contrasting ways in which different media forms deal with similar themes. Film reviews and marketing in print media and on television might make a good example that you can explore.

While you have these texts in front of you or at least in your head, try to think through what you might do in terms of the headings we have given you to work with. You don't even have to write anything down, although it will help. The important things is developing the mode of thinking and the mental agility to make these kinds of connections and to develop your ideas on the hoof.

If you follow this advice you will go to the exam room not only ready for anything that comes up, but also mentally prepared to go into MED6 mode straight from the starting gun.

Let's have a look at an actual pair of texts that have been set for MED6 and consider how you might go about tackling them.

In January 2004, candidates taking MED6 were presented with two print texts. These were:

> *Animals and You*, published by D.C. Thomson & Co. Ltd, April 2002
>
> *Wildlife*, published by BBC Magazines, October 2002.
>
> The front cover and contents page of each of these magazines were issued and these are reproduced on pages. 123–7.

The first job then is to identify similarities and differences.

Both magazines deal with a similar subject matter – animals. Both are monthly magazines available at newsagents. They will be competing within the market of niche interest monthly periodicals, although many will be bought on a subscription basis. There are clear surface differences between the two magazines. First they are obviously directed at different audiences. *Animals and You* states clearly its audience beneath the masthead – 'for cool girls who love animals'. The girl on the front cover holding a rabbit suggests that these cool girls are all pre-teens. *Wildlife* seems to be aimed at a broader demographic. The audience looks to be primarily adult. It is also a spin-off from BBC wildlife programmes. This would suggest it has an appeal to the same audience that might be expected to watch these programmes. You might also detect implicitly a conservation agenda appealing to people who

Figure 7: © DC Thomson and Co., Ltd

**Figure 7 continued**

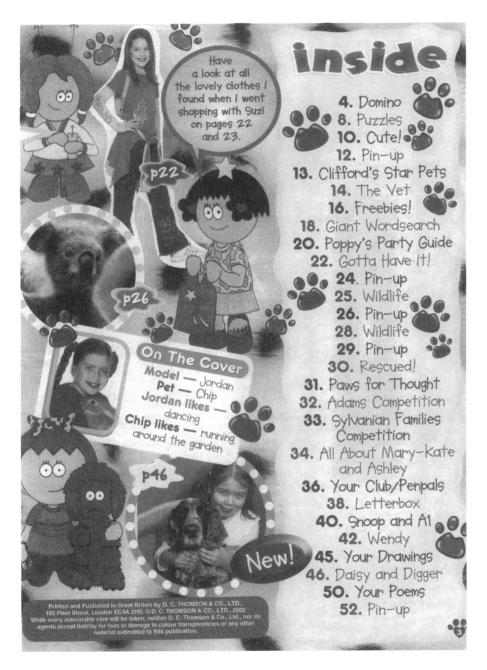

Have a look at all the lovely clothes I found when I went shopping with Suzi on pages 22 and 23.

p22

p26

**On The Cover**
Model — Jordan
Pet — Chip
Jordan likes — dancing
Chip likes — running around the garden

p46

New!

Printed and Published in Great Britain by D. C. THOMSON & CO., LTD., 185 Fleet Street, London EC4A 2HS. © D. C. THOMSON & CO., LTD., 2002 While every reasonable care will be taken, neither D. C. Thomson & Co., Ltd., nor its agents accept liability for loss or damage to colour transparencies or any other material submitted to this publication.

**Figure 7 continued**

Figure 8: © BBC Magazines

# Contents

OCTOBER 2002

NATURE'S TREASURES

Darwin Centre
AT THE NATURAL HISTORY MUSEUM

**FREE INSIDE**

■ COVER: Tiger, by Thomas Mangelsen/Minden Pictures.

**Figure 8 continued**

are concerned about protecting the environment as is evident in the 'News of the Earth' section on the contents page.

Perhaps the fundamental difference is one of representation. In *Animals and You*, animals are represented in close proximity to people. These are mostly tame domestic pets that can be handled and cared for by your girls. The tigress which adorns the cover despite her relaxed pose is clearly a powerful natural force, not something it would be advisable to pick up and pet. She is represented as majestic, powerful and independent.

**NOTE**

> Look out for the danger that is present in these texts and others like them. There is a vast amount of material here – five pages of densely packed text. On no account should you try to explore it all. If you do, you will never get beyond textual analysis in the hour and a half you have available. This really is about being selective in what you choose to comment on. Examiners will also tell that candidates who have a printed text in front of them are likely to spend more time describing it than those who are shown a moving image text and have to work from notes and their memory.

Wider contexts: what do these texts signal as possible areas to explore for wider contexts? Well just as there is a great deal that might be covered in terms of textual analysis, so there is a great deal in terms of wider contexts. Be careful that you do not end up skating superficially over a wider area at the expense of some detailed digging into specific issues.

First there is the issue of audience. Both magazines are examples of texts aimed at niche markets. The first is determined by age, gender and interest, the second primarily by interest. Note also the intertextual nature of *Wildlife* and its symbiotic relationship with BBC television programmes. You may also want to make a brief excursion into institutional contexts at this point in terms of D.C. Thomson and the BBC's broader publishing interests in a range of niche markets.

Clearly the issue of animals and how they are represented in the media is calling out to be addressed. You might note that even in the rather serious and upmarket *Wildlife* magazine we were teased to read about 'Secrets of a tigress: Her sons and her lovers'. Wild animals are provided with a human narrative perspective to encourage the audience to empathise with them. Similarly in *Animals and You*, animals are framed as cute lifestyle accessories for trendy young girls.

"**On the Cover**

**Model – Jordan**

**Pet – Chip**

**Jordan Likes – dancing**

**Chip Likes – running around the garden**"

In both magazines you might identify that ideological forces are at play. The heavy emphasis in both is about 'caring'. In *Wildlife* we are encouraged to find out about and care for the environment and the many species of animal that roam our planet. In *Animals and You* the focus of care is our domestic pets. In several ways this magazine is typical of many that are targeted at the female market of all ages. Caring, loving and nurturing are seen as essential skills that a girl must develop if she is to fulfil her role in society.

## Theories

Clearly there is a feminist take on both texts: the tigress situated in her role as sexual partner and mother, the training manual for your girls to learn their social roles. You can certainly expand these ideas both through the texts you have here and the wider magazine publishing market.

Uses and gratifications would be an interesting idea to explore particularly in relation to *Wildlife*. What are the uses and gratifications to which we put this type of magazine? Similarly what has stimulated our interest in the media consumption of wildlife? Most of the features in *Wildlife* are about other people's experiences, often potentially dangerous and remote ones. You might wish to explore the way in which texts of this type offer us such experiences without leaving the comfort of our armchairs.

You might want to consider some elements of the 'effects debate' into the nature of the effects of *Animals and You* on the your female readership in terms of the impact of this and similar media texts as agencies for socialisation and the allocation of gender roles within a patriarchy.

Here is an extract from the Chief Examiner's report for this exam. A Chief Examiner's report is produced to report to teachers how candidates performed in the examination. You might find it useful reading.

Candidates should be reminded that the demands for this unit are significantly different from those for MED1. There was clearly a temptation with print texts sitting in front of candidates that they would feel the need to deconstruct the media language employed in these texts in some depth. Centres are reminded that the ability to deconstruct a media text in terms of the basic key concepts is tested in MED1 and cannot be rewarded highly at this level. Where candidates structured their argument around demonstrating how the text was constructed to target a particular audience and did not move beyond the basic key concepts of Media Language, Audience and Representation they could not be highly rewarded.

Centres should remember that it is not possible for candidates to access the top mark bands for this unit unless they engage with media issues and debates and demonstrate a knowledge and understanding of the wider contexts of production for the two texts. There were many opportunities for candidates to explore the wider contexts of production with these texts. The BBC was an obvious context, but candidates might have been aware of the position of D.C. Thomson in the marketplace as well. There were certainly opportunities for candidates to explore social contexts and to discus the ideologies of *Animals and You* as a lifestyle magazine with an animal 'pretext', for example. Given the wide range of articles offered by the magazine, the use of celebrities and the emphasis on shopping for clothes for example, together with the representations of ideal role models for the audience to aspire to, the premise is wider than simply 'pets'. Strong candidates were also able to discuss the representation of the 'human qualities' of the tigress to interpolate the audience to respond in a particular way, and to write in some depth about the way this was being marketed and the social context for the need to 'dumb down' the content to appeal to a wider market.

Candidates taking the MED6 exam in June 2005 were confronted with an interesting pairing of texts. Both were moving image texts. The first was an extract from a programme called *Regency House Party* which had been broadcast on Channel 4 on Saturday evening in March 2004. The second was an extract from *SAS: Are you tough enough* (third series) which was first broadcast on BBC2 on the following Sunday evening in March 2004. The two texts ran for a total of approximately six minutes.

The common and most obvious link between both programmes is that they were variations on the theme of reality television which you will recognise as a popular genre both with television producers and with audiences. Interestingly neither programme seems to have achieved a particularly high profile, so presumably unlike *Big Brother* and *I'm a Celebrity Get Me Out Of Here*, the format proved less than successful in terms of audience ratings.

With any luck you should notice immediately that establishing this link between the two texts has opened up to us a whole world of potential opportunities to explore wider contexts, theoretical perspectives and media issues. Be cautious, however, because you need also to realise that there is a great danger opening up in front of you – it would be very easy to move swiftly on from the texts and write an essay which is in essence 'everything I have always wanted to say about reality television programmes'. Clearly this is a temptation which you need to resist, even though these texts present opportunities within your response to engage to some degree with the debate about reality television and even wider issues of dumbing down of television output.

A good response to this task will be constantly supporting the points being made with reference back to the texts themselves. It will show a clear grasp of engaging with media texts within an appropriate contextual framework and demonstrate a clear grasp of wider contexts and theoretical perspectives. So the plan that you might come up with for a response to a question of this sort would be something along the following lines.

Similarities: both are variations on the reality television format in which there is a high degree of participation by members of the audience. Both are shown at prime time weekend viewing slots on minority channels with a commitment to 'quality' programming of interest to minority groups and yet seem remarkably downmarket and mainstream. *Regency House Party* has elements of costume drama, which television once did very well particularly in the serialisation of novels, Jane Austen's for example. There is evidence of hybridity within each text as it seems to draw on more than one genre for its appeal. *SAS* is seemingly laddish but also interestingly has at least one female contestant in order to maintain some sense of political correctness presumably.

Wider contexts: it is important that we are seeing yet another spin on the well-worn reality format, but not on this occasion lavish productions involving purpose-built sets and D list celebrity participants. It is unlikely to attract mass audience despite its prime time slot. *Regency House Party* is competing with Saturday evening prime time on mass appeal channels BBC1 and ITV1. Production costs are a clear factor in the production of such formats as is audience appeal. *Regency House Party* is likely to appeal to a niche audience of people who might be interested in house parties and period drama perhaps. There are clearly opportunities to consider the impact of the 'digital revolution' and the increase in reality television output.

Theoretical perspectives, uses and gratifications: audience participation and seeming empowerment contribute to influencing programme narrative outcomes as well as participating in them. The postmodern perspectives of *Regency House Party* are concerned with the breaking of the high–low culture divide by taking elements of elite culture and fusing them with mass entertainment game show format. There is the possible exploration of issues relating to the sanitising of war and the ideological function of *SAS: Are you tough enough?* appealing to notions of heroism and jingoism at a time when the country was at war.

Finally let us consider an interesting pairing of texts set in June 2004. The first text was an extract from *Smash Hits* magazine published by EMAP in October 2002, entitled 'The School of Hard Knocks'. This article from this magazine can be seen opposite. The second text was a video extract. It comprised a CBBC report on the programme *Fame Academy* broadcast by the BBC in October 2002.

The second text showed a young link man introducing two presenters, Jake and Holly, who were fronting a live update on what had been happening at *Fame Academy*. The two introduce themselves seated in two shot by waving manically and shouting 'Hello' to the camera. They immediately reiterate that the broadcast is live, a fact further reinforced by the 'live icon' at the top right of the screen. Both presenters are young and brightly dressed as befits a children's television person-ality. They readily adopt the zany patronising attitude that young children clearly appreciate.

We are then shown an extract from the title sequence of *Fame Academy*, a very stylised series of shots involving dancing and holding hands. Jake explains that this has been a day of high drama because one of the *Fame Academy* members, Naomi, has been asked to leave because of a nodule on her throat. Helpfully he indicates the location of his own throat to reinforce and clarify the message.

Figure 9: © EMAP

There has been a dramatic moment when she leaves and Holly was sent to record this for posterity. We are then presented with the actuality of this event. First inside the house the contestants say an emotional and tactile farewell to Naomi. This involved a great deal of demonstrative luvvie-type hugging. We then cut to an exterior shot where Holly is waiting with her polaroid camera. As the car carrying Naomi speeds by, Holly tries unsuccessfully it seems to take a photograph through the windows in much the same way that the paparazzi take shots of celebrities speeding away from media attention, or criminals being escorted to prison in the backs of vans. At this point the extract ends.

It is interesting to note that candidates were on this occasion asked to consider texts from different media: a magazine and a television programme. When this happens it is clear that we are looking for a common theme between the two texts. In this case it is the fact that they both refer to *Fame Academy*, the BBC's own version of a reality television show in the *Pop Idol* mould. You should by now have racing through your mind a number of potential directions in which you might take an answer based on these texts. No doubt many of these will be centred on the nature of reality television and shows like *Fame Academy*, *Pop Idol* and *X Factor* in which people hoping for a career in the music industry get their chance to develop their talents in front of the television cameras.

> **NOTE**
>
> A word of caution: remember texts like this should not be taken as an opportunity to write down everything you know about reality television shows. Remember that you should try to link back your ideas to the texts that have been set. They are both a starting point and to some extent a reference point throughout your essay.

First off you might like to consider the important concept of intertextuality. Both texts rely for their impact on the audience's knowledge of and interest in *Fame Academy*. This idea of promotion of texts through other texts can provide an interesting postmodern perspective of the media feeding off itself. This allows you to develop some potentially interesting ideas that might link to a postmodern perspective more broadly. For example you might like to consider the way in which the CBBC programme incorporates many of the elements of news reporting in order to give the impression of a dramatic narrative unfolding.

*Make a list of some of the ways in which a postmodern perspective might lend theoretical light to these texts.*

You also need to explore some of the wider contexts that are at play here. One of these might be linked to the idea of a media-saturated society. Programmes like *Fame Academy* are clearly created to fill air time. They do this not only through their own broadcast slots but also by filling space in other programmes, of which this CBBC report is a prime example. Similarly they provide copy to fill up magazine space as in *Smash Hits*.

You might also consider how the market for both texts is an audience of children. This has important ideological implications for the social values implicit in the message, particularly in terms of what our society seeks to reward people for achieving.

Perhaps you might also want to write about the fact that the video extract is from the BBC, as is the *Fame Academy* programme. The BBC is clearly following a trend established by *Pop Idol* on the commercial channel, ITV. How far can the BBC be accused of dumbing down in order to chase audience ratings?

You should see from the above that we have immediately suggested to you three or four directions in which we might take a response to these texts. Find yourself a couple of contemporary texts that deal with a similar theme and plan out in note form your own response to them.

In the section on revision we suggested that one way of preparing for the MED6 exam was to find texts that you think might pair together in an interesting way and then to subject them to the MED6 treatment outlined above. Here are suggestions for the types of texts on which you might try this out.

- Newspapers aimed at different markets, national and local or popular and quality
- Posters for films of different or similar genres
- Trailers for similar television programmes
- Magazine articles and television reports covering a similar topic

## SAMPLE PAGE 2 OF THE AQA A2 MEDIA STUDIES MED6 EXAMINATION

---

2

---

**Texts** ──

The texts for this paper are:

> First the texts you will be using are identified. Note that useful information is given here that identifies the context for the texts for you. You may need to use this in your answer. Note also that some texts will be in different formats, e.g a video text and a print text. Print texts are usually included as a supplementary booklet.

**Text One** – The front cover and contents pages of the magazine *Animals and You*, published by D.C. THOMSON & CO. LTD, April 2002.

**Text Two** – The front cover and contents page of the magazine *BBC Wildlife*, published by BBC Magazines, October 2002.

> Note the instructions. There is nothing to stop you writing your answer straight away. You would be a fool to do so though. Use the 30 minutes of note taking to engage fully with the texts and identify those elusive wider contexts and theoretical perspectives. Don't forget to write these notes in your answer book and cross through them so that they are not marked.

**Instructions**

You should spend 30 minutes reading these texts and making notes on **both** texts. You then have **one hour** to complete this task.

**Task** ──

Using the comparison of these two texts as your starting point, explore the media issues and debates which they raise.

In your answer you will need to address:

- Key Concepts

- Contextual Factors

- Media Theory.

> The wording of the task is crucial. Comparison is a starting point, not the main focus of the question. The main focus is to 'explore the media issues and debates which they raise'. If you get your head round this, you will do well. If you don't, you won't. Note that below the question is a series of bullet points given as handholds. If you have prepared well, you won't need these, but they are a useful reminder.

*(60 marks)*

**END OF QUESTION**

Acknowledgement of copyright holders and publishers

**Text One**: *Animals and You*, published by D.C. Thomson & Co. Ltd, April 2002.
**Text Two**: *BBC Wildlife Magazine*, published by BBC Magazines, October 2002.

# SAMPLE MARK SCHEME FOR THE AQA A2 MEDIA STUDIES MED6 EXAMINATION

**General Marking Criteria**

**Level 6   51 – 60 marks**

> You can show your ability to make judgements independently using the theories and conceptual understanding you have gleaned from studying the media.

> You need to show off what you have learned throughout the course.

> You need to say intelligent things about the wider contexts that these texts throw up.

Candidates make extensive use of their learning at AS and A2 levels in responding to the texts, with sophisticated knowledge and application of wider contexts relevant to the materials.

Very good evidence of critical autonomy - the ability to make individual judgements informed by relevant theories, issues and debates.

> Synoptic is a key word for A2. It means pulling things together, especially in terms of the theory.

Evidence of a very good synoptic ability (drawing together theories, issues and debates from different parts of the specification) in making effective textual readings and comparisons based on a comprehensive understanding and application of all relevant Key Concepts.

> You can compare these texts using all the Key Concepts that might apply to them.

Candidates show a sophisticated identification of the similarities and differences between the two texts, in a well structured and engaged response showing a very clear understanding of the form and function of the different materials.

> What you write is well-structured, logical and makes sense.

> You can identify the issues that link these texts.

> You know why these texts are like they are and what they are intended for.

**Level 5   41 – 50 marks**

Candidates make use of their learning at AS and A2 levels in responding to the texts, with good knowledge and application of wider contexts relevant to the materials.

There is also good evidence of critical autonomy - the ability to make individual judgements informed by relevant theories, issues and debates.

Evidence of a good synoptic ability (drawing together theories, issues and debates from different parts of the specification) in making effective textual readings and comparisons based on a clear understanding and application of all relevant Key Concepts.

Candidates show a good identification of the similarities and differences between the two texts, in a fluent and engaged response showing a clear understanding of the form and function of the different materials.

> This is the top level of the MED6 mark scheme. If you produce an answer that fulfils these criteria you should score between 51 and 60 marks.

**Level 4   31 – 40 marks**

Candidates make some use of their learning at AS and A2 levels in responding to the texts, with sound knowledge and application of some wider contexts relevant to the materials.

There is also a reasonable sense of critical autonomy - the ability to make individual judgements informed by relevant theories, issues and debates.

Evidence of some synoptic ability (drawing together theories, issues and debates from different parts of the specification) in making textual readings and comparisons, although possibly not fully developed, based on a sound understanding and application of most relevant Key Concepts.

Candidates show a sound identification of the similarities and differences between the two texts, in a structured response showing some understanding of the form and function of the different materials, although they may concentrate on some parts of the texts to the exclusion of others.

Reproduced by kind permission of the Assessment and Qualifications Alliance.

# CONCLUSION

## RESOURCES

How you use the many resources available to you in preparing for your A2 exams will depend on the stage you are at. If you are doing last-minute revision trying to make up for not having got your head round the course in the past year, then it is probably best to stick to just using this book and whatever notes and information you have gleaned along the way. On the other hand if you are using this book as part of a planned campaign of revision, there are a number of places you can go to find additional support.

The first of these is the A2 textbook in the Routledge Essentials series, Bennett, P., Slater, J. and Wall, P. (2005) *A2 Media Studies, The Essential Introduction*, Routledge. This book is especially written with the AQA A2 specification in mind, so it covers all the key elements of both written papers as well as the Independent Study. We suggest that you dip into it to help fill in any gaps in your understanding and knowledge in relation to both MED4 and MED6.

There are other A level textbooks that you should have a look at if you have time, although you will have to be selective in choosing the sections that will help. Have a quick check of the contents list and index to see how much of the topics you need they cover. A book like O'Sullivan, T., Dutton B. and Rayner P. *Studying the Media*, Hodder, covers many of the concepts you need for study at this level and is recommended both as a reference source and background reading.

Of course there is a vast amount of information available on the web to help and support you. However, you really do need to be discriminating to get anything useful out of it. It is very easy to waste a lot of time randomly following links. At this stage you probably don't have the time to spare doing this.

There are a number of schools and colleges that offer access to Media Studies sites designed to help their own students taking the AQA specification. As these tend to change over a period of time, it is not possible to make specific recommendations, but it is worth spending some time seeking them out and checking to see if there is material that can help you.

There are, however, a number of established sites that can be particularly helpful, such as the sites of the regulatory bodies that control the media. Certainly the OFCOM site (www.ofcom.org.uk), Press Complaints Commission site (www.pcc.org.uk) and the Advertising Standards Authority (www.asa.org.uk) are worth bearing in mind for quick reference and perhaps to stimulate some ideas for revision topics.

The BBC's own site is a vast resource that you can tap into in many ways. Other reference sites can provide useful support. The Internet Movies Database (http://uk.imdb.com/) has handy links to provide quickly accessed information about films, their directors and stars. Beware though if you are interested in film, it can become addictive. TV ARK (www.tv-ark.org.uk/) provides a comprehensive back catalogue of clips from television programmes that may provide interesting background material most especially to genre.

Increasingly the awarding bodies and QCA itself are facing up to their responsibilities and providing support via their website for candidates. You can if you wish get in touch with the 'Exams Doctor' at QCA if you feel that you are in need of support. 'Dr A Level' smiles benignly from his home page at http://www.qca.org.uk/11449.html and even invites you to email him with any queries you may have.

Similarly the BBC's guide H2G2 to Life the Universe and Everything has some suggestions for revision and taking exams. You need to follow the links from http://www.bbc.co.uk/dna/h2g2/C521. The BBC Radio 1 website has some links to exam issues including advice on dealing with stress. The links are posted on: http://www.bbc.co.uk/radio1/onelife/education/index.shtml?exams#topics.

Finally the AQA website has some information about preparing for and taking exams. You need to navigate from: http://www.aqa.org.uk/over/advice/index.html

A lot of this stuff is pretty self-evident, but it is often the simple truths you need to hear when you are getting ready for an exam. In the midst of all this, don't forget that the very best resource you have is yourself. A level Media Studies is about your own ability and willingness to enquire and to question. Learn how to do this and you will do well.

## SO NOW IT'S UP TO YOU

We hope that you have found this book useful. Obviously there are many reasons that you have chosen to read it. You may simply want to go into the A2 exams with the very best possible preparation. On the other hand this book may have been your last chance to make up for some ropey preparation, a last ditch effort to dig yourself out a hole.

Whatever reason you have for reading this book, we hope you have tried to use it positively. Remember too to try to think beyond the exam and remind yourself of some of the pleasures that media texts have given you. Indeed it can be argued that the more you enjoy the texts you have studied, the more you will have engaged with them. It is this level of engagement that is often the key to your success in A level examinations. Examiners will always reward enthusiasm and engagement with texts especially when it is closely allied to a grasp of key media concepts.

Writing revision books is potentially a cynical business, so one thing we hope is that this book will have had for you a value beyond merely getting you through your exam. You will we hope have noted in both this book and its AS companion that we have placed a lot of emphasis on both individual research and independence of thought. We have also argued that the ability and willingness to question the received wisdom of media theory is to be encouraged.

Interestingly, these are all qualities that are needed if you are to be successful in the next stage of your career, be it a degree course or a job. If you have learned to work independently and form your own opinions based on sound empirical evidence, you should do well significantly beyond the demands of A level exams.

Of course, some of you may well end up working in the media industries themselves. Here the capacity to work independently and to ask difficult questions is the keystone to success in many sectors.

So may we take this opportunity to wish you every success not only in your forthcoming Media Studies exams but also in the career you eventually choose to pursue.

# APPENDIX

## THE EXAM SYSTEM EXPLAINED

Exam papers are set by a Principal Examiner (PE). S/he is usually, although not always, a practising teacher with expertise in the subject. It is the Principal Examiner's job to prepare an initial draft of the examination paper, often as much as 18 months before the paper is to be sat. The Principal Examiner has to set a paper which reflects the demands of the unit that is being examined. If you want to know exactly what the requirements of an individual unit are, then you can look in the specification (always available online) to check this. The PE must produce a paper that is limited to the topics in the specification. S/he must not ask questions that are outside the scope of what is written in the specification. You can see from this that the specification provides you with a useful guide to exactly what you need to know in order to pass the exam.

In setting the paper the PE must also bear in mind what questions have been set on past papers. S/he must perform a balancing act which makes sure that the paper is in line with those of previous series but is itself a new and different paper. There is also an onus on the PE to ensure that over a period of time, all the topics set out in the specification are covered. Of course, second guessing what is going to be on a paper is a dangerous game, but it is worth bearing in mind that if a topic has not appeared for a few series, it might well be due.

Once the PE has completed a draft of the paper complete with a mark scheme (more on this later) it is sent off to a person called the Reviser. The Reviser is another senior examiner, again usually a practising teacher with subject expertise. The Reviser's job is to consider the paper to ensure that it is accessible to candidates, that it is fair and that it reflects the demands of the specification. This means that all the questions on the paper must relate closely to what is in the specification. The Reviser may suggest changes to the paper, either in just the wording of a question, through to replacing one or more questions that may be considered inappropriate. An exam paper usually results from extensive discussion or even an argument between the PE and the Reviser.

This, however, is not the end of the process – far from it. The papers agreed by the PE and the Reviser are now produced in the same format that they will appear on your desk in the exam room. Prior to this they have merely been produced as drafts. The next stage is for the papers to be taken to a Question Paper Evaluation Committee, or QPEC. The QPEC consists of a Chair of Examiners, the Principal Examiners and Revisers of papers which are being considered, a Subject Adviser, usually another practising subject specialist teacher, as well as the Subject Officer from the exam board, who looks after the administration of Media Studies for AQA.

The job is of these people is to look carefully at the paper again and to do much the same job as the Reviser did previously:

1   Ensure the paper is in line with the demands of the specification

2   Make sure the questions are worded so that they are not ambiguous or confusing to candidates in any way

3   Satisfy themselves that the paper is fair to candidates at all different levels of ability

4   Consider the paper in light of those set in previous series

5   Consider the paper in light of other Media Studies papers likely to be taken by candidates during their course

It is only after the QPEC are satisfied with the paper that it can move on to the next stage which introduces another key player in the paper setting process – the Scrutineer. The Scrutineer's job is to act as the last line of defence in ensuring that the paper is fair accurate and correct in all details. The Scrutineer is in fact expected to Scrutinise the paper by actually sitting down and attempting it. Although this may not quite happen literally, not least because of the length of time it would take to cover all the different combinations of questions possible, the Scrutineer is expected to place himself or herself in the position of a candidate taking the paper. In doing so, it is intended that s/he will reveal any hidden flaws or problems with the paper not identified by the QPEC. The Scrutineer is also expected to check how effective the mark scheme is likely to be in light of their scrutiny of the paper and highlight any deficiencies. If this scrutiny of the paper does reveal any problems, the paper is sent back to the PE to look at again.

Assuming that everyone who has seen the paper is now satisfied, the paper now goes through a series of proof stages, again being carefully checked at each one, until it is finally ready for print and distribution to centres, where exams officers are expected to keep it under lock and key until the day of the exam.

As you will have seen, the exam setting process is a careful and deliberate one with clearly defined rules to establish the protocol for setting a paper. This is important if mistakes are to be avoided. A mistake on an exam paper can obviously have serious repercussions for candidates as well as examiners and exam boards.

One important issue from all of this is to consider what it means for you as a candidate. Well apart from ensuring that the paper which you receive in the exam room is as fair and error free as possible, you might also like to think about some of the parameters by which examiners are bound when they set your paper. Notice that we identified a number of points about the paper setting process. For candidates, the important ones are:

1   The paper you sit must be limited to the topics in the specification. Check with your copy of the specification to be sure you know exactly what these topics are. They are given under the heading of Content for each of the A2 units and consist of a series of bullet points identifying the areas that you need to cover.

2   All topics in the specification should be covered over a period of time. What this means is that you can look back over the past three or four series of exam papers for a unit, most usefully MED4, and identify topics that have been popular and those that may not have appeared for a while. Of course, there would be a huge element of risk about gambling on a specific questions coming up perhaps because they had not been set for a while, but you can at least look to see which bullet points in the content are popular and which are less so.

3   The paper must be different from those set in previous series. Similarly it is worth looking at the most recent past paper to see what sort of questions were set last time. Again, it would be a big gamble to assume that recent items from the content will not reappear, albeit in a slightly different guise.

4   The paper is likely, however, to follow the same style and format as those set in previous series unless the exam board had announced anything to the contrary. So for example on MED4 you can expect to have pairs of EITHER OR questions because this format has been established over a period of time.

NOTE

Despite the carefully orchestrated process for setting exam papers and the many safeguards that are in place, it is still possible for errors to occur on a paper. If you think there is an error on the paper or there is any unforeseen problem with the paper, alert the invigilator to this. Don't be afraid to do this, but at least make sure that you do it quietly and discreetly without alarming all the people around you. If the invigilator has to go away and make enquiries, get on with those bits of the paper that are not problematic. Whatever you do, don't just sit back and wait for an answer. The chances of a serious problem with the paper as you can see from the information above are pretty remote.

## WHAT HAPPENS TO YOUR EXAM SCRIPT WHEN YOU HAVE FINISHED THE EXAM?

Most students breathe a great sigh of relief once they have completed their exam and then spend several weeks anxiously waiting for the result to drop through their letterbox. Few give any real thought to what goes on after the invigilator has collected their exam script. It is worth pausing for a few moments to find out about this process, not least because the insight it provides can prove useful in helping you in both preparing for and taking exams.

Each centre's exam scripts are collected by your exams officer and sent to a designated examiner. Usually each paper is marked by a different examiner except occasionally in subjects where there are very few candidates. The examiner's job is to mark the scripts and send in the marks to the exam board, either online or on a mark sheet which can be read by a computer. So how does an examiner arrive at a mark for your script?

Well first it is important that you understand the hierarchical nature of the examination system. As you will have realised from reading the section on setting exam papers, senior examiners are generally practising teachers with a specialism in the subject they examine. This means that setting and marking exams is a part-time job for them. Exam boards employ full-time staff who are responsible for the day to say running of the exam system. Probably the most important of these is the Subject Officer, who is directly responsible for overseeing the setting and marking of exams in one or more subjects. Subject officers are required to convene and attend all the key meetings during the year for their subject.

The setting and marking of each paper is the responsibility of a Principal Examiner. One of the PEs or Principal Moderators, who look after the coursework units, will also act as Chief Examiner ultimately responsible for all of the units in a particular qualification.

Once the exam scripts have been collected in, the Subject Officer convenes a standardising meeting for each unit. The purpose of this meeting is to explain the marking process to all of the examiners and to set a standard to which they are all required to mark. If the number of candidates entering for the unit is more than a couple of thousand, the standardising meeting will be preceded by a pre-standardising meeting. The reason for this is that the PE will have the support of one or more senior examiners, also known as team leaders (TLs). These TLs will be experienced examiners each given the job of supervising their own team of examiners. At the pre-standardising meeting, the PE and the TLs will consider a range of scripts and give each one a mark in line with the mark scheme. Ultimately it is the judgement of the PE which carries the most weight. S/he is responsible for setting the standard of the marking and in an ideal world every script that is marked will be to exactly the same standard as though the PE had marked it themselves. The standardising process then is about the PE ensuring that the marking of so-called 'assistants' is to a uniform standard set by him or herself.

One of the many changes that have taken place in the exam system over the past ten years or so is the increased demands on exam boards for transparency. This means that the assessment system you are about to submit yourself to has to be fair and open. Transparency implies this fairness and openness by suggesting that it should be easy to see into the examining process at all stages to ensure that it is fair. Although it would be unreasonable to suggest that the system is wholly transparent, there is a lot of evidence to show that it has moved significantly in this direction. The return of marked scripts is one good example of this transparency in action. Another is the fact that mark schemes for all exams are now available on the boards' websites. Unfortunately for candidates these are mark schemes from past papers rather than the ones you will be taking, but they should still be useful to you in a number of ways.

Let us consider some of the ways in which looking at mark schemes might help you. As you will have read on page 144 mark schemes are written by the Principal Examiner and are designed to be used by examiners to mark scripts in their allocation. Clearly one of their functions is to identify the qualities that an examiner should expect to find in scripts at the different standards of achievement attained by candidates. The mark schemes for MED4 and MED6 are divided into levels with those giving the highest marks at the top. The highest level is the one that you should be focused on. Ideally it describes the type of script that you are likely to produce in your examination. Even if in reality it doesn't, it should identify for you the standard of work that you should attempt to produce for each of your answers in the exam. The closer you can get to this quality of response, the higher should be your grade.

The process by which each assistant examiner is standardised is a rigorous one. At the standardising meeting itself, examiners will be expected to consider at least half a dozen scripts covering all the possible questions that candidates might have attempted from the paper. Each individual question will be marked by each examiner with careful reference to the mark scheme. The mark they arrived at will be compared to the mark given by the PE and agreed by the TLs. Where an examiner arrives at a mark different from the one agreed, his or her TL will spend time discussing how the difference may have occurred and explaining by means of the mark scheme how the PE's mark was arrived at. By the end of the standardising meeting each assistant examiner's mark should be in line with the standard set by the PE.

Of course this is not the end of the process – far from it! As soon as an assistant examiner returns home from the standardising meeting, s/he will start marking the pile of scripts they have been allocated.

> **NOTE**
>
> ALLOCATION: Each examiner is expected to mark around 300 scripts for an individual unit. Some examiners mark more than one unit and some examiners mark several different units for different exam boards or in different subjects.

As soon as the assistant examiner has marked a number of scripts s/he has to send a sample of ten scripts to his/her TL for checking. This sample is expected to reflect a range of marks scored by candidates to ensure that the examiner is confident with all levels of the mark scheme, not just say the higher end or the bottom. It is the TL's job to re-mark the sample in line with the standard established by the PE.

> **NOTE**
>
> TLs have to submit themselves to exactly the same process as assistant examiners. On this occasion, the PE checks their sample to make sure that their own marking is in line with that set at the standardisation meeting. A TL cannot check another examiner's marking until the PE has confirmed that they are marking to the correct standard.

Assuming that the assistant examiner's marking is accurate, i.e. in close agreement with the TLs, s/he is 'cleared' to carry on marking the rest of the scripts allocated. If the TL is not happy with the marking of the sample received, then the AE will be asked to provide an additional sample after discussing with the TL where the marking has gone wrong. If this second sample is correctly marked, then the AE is cleared to proceed with marking. If, as sometimes happens, the AE's marking is not sufficiently accurate, s/he will be asked to stop any further marking and return all scripts to the exam board.

As you can see this is quite a rigorous process to ensure that all examiners are marking accurately and to the established standard. If an examiner is allowed to carry on marking without having a very clear idea of the standard, then a lot of candidates can potentially get the wrong mark for their exam.

Of course this is not the end of the checking process. Other important checks are also in place.

All TLs and AEs will have further scripts checked as part of a quality control process. This is done by:

- A further sample being checked halfway through the exam process
- A review of examiners' scripts by senior examiners at the exam board office at the end of the marking process
- A statistical check to see how closely the examiner's marking is to that of other examiners by comparing statistical evidence such as the mean mark and the standard deviation
- A check where the grade predicted by your teacher is significantly higher than the mark your script has been given

As you can see there are a whole series of checks that take place to ensure that an examiner is marking to the proper standard. However, despite such careful checking it is still possible for things to go wrong not least because the process relies on human beings capable of making mistakes. In the next section we look at what happens when you get your results. As you will be aware, this result is not necessarily the end of the process as it is still possible to ask for your script to undergo further checks.

**NOTE**

Assistant examiners are told at the standardising meeting that they must read every script carefully in order to award marks. You can make it easier for the examiner by paying careful attention to how your script looks when it arrives on the examiner's desk. Make sure you:

- Write clearly and as legibly as possible. Having a good pen with blue or black ink will help. If your handwriting is truly awful, consider printing.
- Make it absolutely clear which question you are answering. It is a good idea to start each new question on a new page of your exam booklet. Clearly indicate the question by writing the number of the question, e.g. 3a, in the margin or writing out the question in full.

NOTE

- Paragraph your work properly. This helps break up your answer into logical sections. A whole page of handwriting with no breaks is a daunting prospect for even the most seasoned of examiners.
- Avoid using correcting fluid (not allowed by exam boards because it sticks pages together) and pens other than blue and black.
- Use helpful signposts for the examiner, e.g. put quotes on a separate line, perhaps.

Of course, even if you have written very clearly with your very best pen and followed all of the guidance above, you may still end up being disappointed with your result. On the other hand you may be very pleasantly surprised or even astounded. In the latter case you will probably decide not to get your result changed; in the former case you might. So what do you do if you think the examiners have got it wrong?

Well all exam boards are required to provide an 'enquiries upon results' service. This means that if you think your exam paper has been marked incorrectly, there is the facility available to check it. Inevitably it is not quite as simple as that; if you appeal against your grade and you are wrong it will cost you money, about £40 in the case of a re-mark of an A2 unit. There is a time limit on this as well, so you need to act quickly. The other important thing you need to know is that your school or college has to make the request for a re-mark on your behalf. They can only do so if you agree because your grades can potentially go down if the re-mark reveals you have been marked too generously.

So what is involved in a re-mark. Well yet again the AQA website provides you with useful up-to-date information about the procedure but there are two different types of check you can ask for. The first is a basic clerical check to make sure that the marks on your paper have been added up correctly. In the case of MED4 and MED6 this is probably a waste of time and money, given the very small number of marks to be added up. The other possibility is a full re-mark. This means that a senior examiner will be asked to remark your paper to check the accuracy of the original mark. Senior examiners do this fairly and objectively, neither seeking to defend the original mark or to try to find you extra marks. They do this marking as though they were assessing your script for the first time.

It is very likely you may have a university place or job resting on the result of your A2 exam, so you can ask for the priority enquiries service which is a little more expensive. This means that by paying extra, your script will be remarked within 20 days.

One thing you may consider doing is paying for access to your script. You can either do this as part of the enquiries service or separately. You will then receive from the exam board a photocopy of your script with all the marks and annotations that the examiner and possibly a senior examiner have written on it. This may or may not be useful to you. The real potential value of having access to your script is so that you check to see that the mark scheme has been applied fairly. (See section on marks schemes.) It may well be that this is a bit difficult for you to do yourself, so you will probably have to enlist the help of your teacher or another Media Studies specialist, ideally someone used to marking exam scripts. What they will have to do is their own re-mark of the script to see if they sense that the mark you have been awarded is fair or not.

If they don't and you have had your re-mark and the exam board are adamant that they think your mark is fair or have even reduced it, there are still two things you can do:

1   Give up

2   Ask you school to take your case to appeal

What does an appeal involve? Basically an appeal is a two-part process. First an internal investigation is set up at the exam board with an independent scrutineer appointed to look at the issues surrounding the marking of your script. If this process fails to bring a satisfactory resolution, your school can take the case to an external appeal through the Examinations Appeals Board. Full details of the process can be found on the EAB website (http://www.theeab.org.uk/). One thing to bear in mind though is that this appeals process can take a long time and that the number of cases that actually end up at appeal are comparatively few. Most are resolved by the awarding bodies themselves long before this stage is reached.